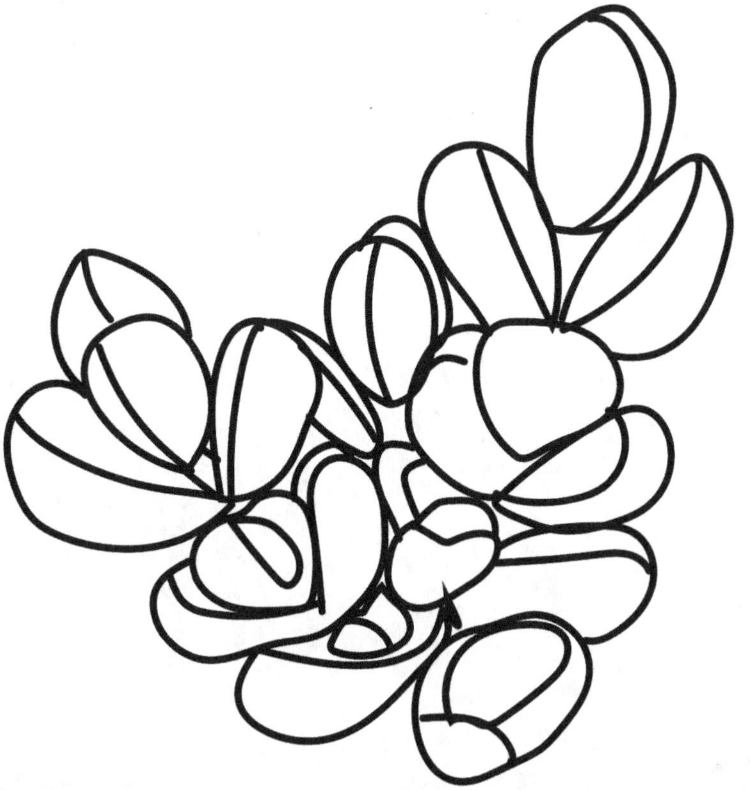

PLANTS

THE COLORING BOOK

CincyPet Media, LLC
PO Box 428686
Cincinnati, OH 45242

www.cincypetmag.com

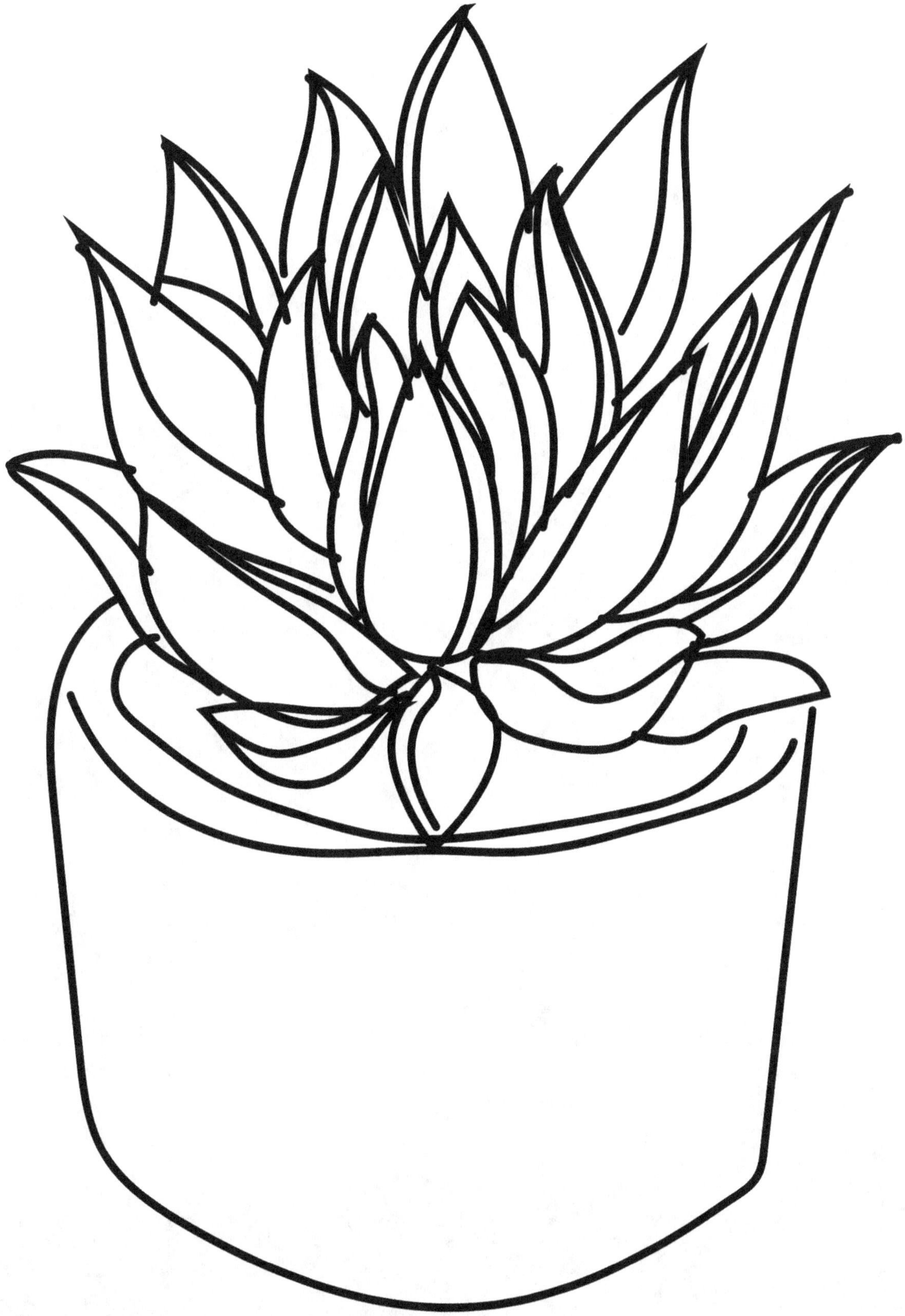

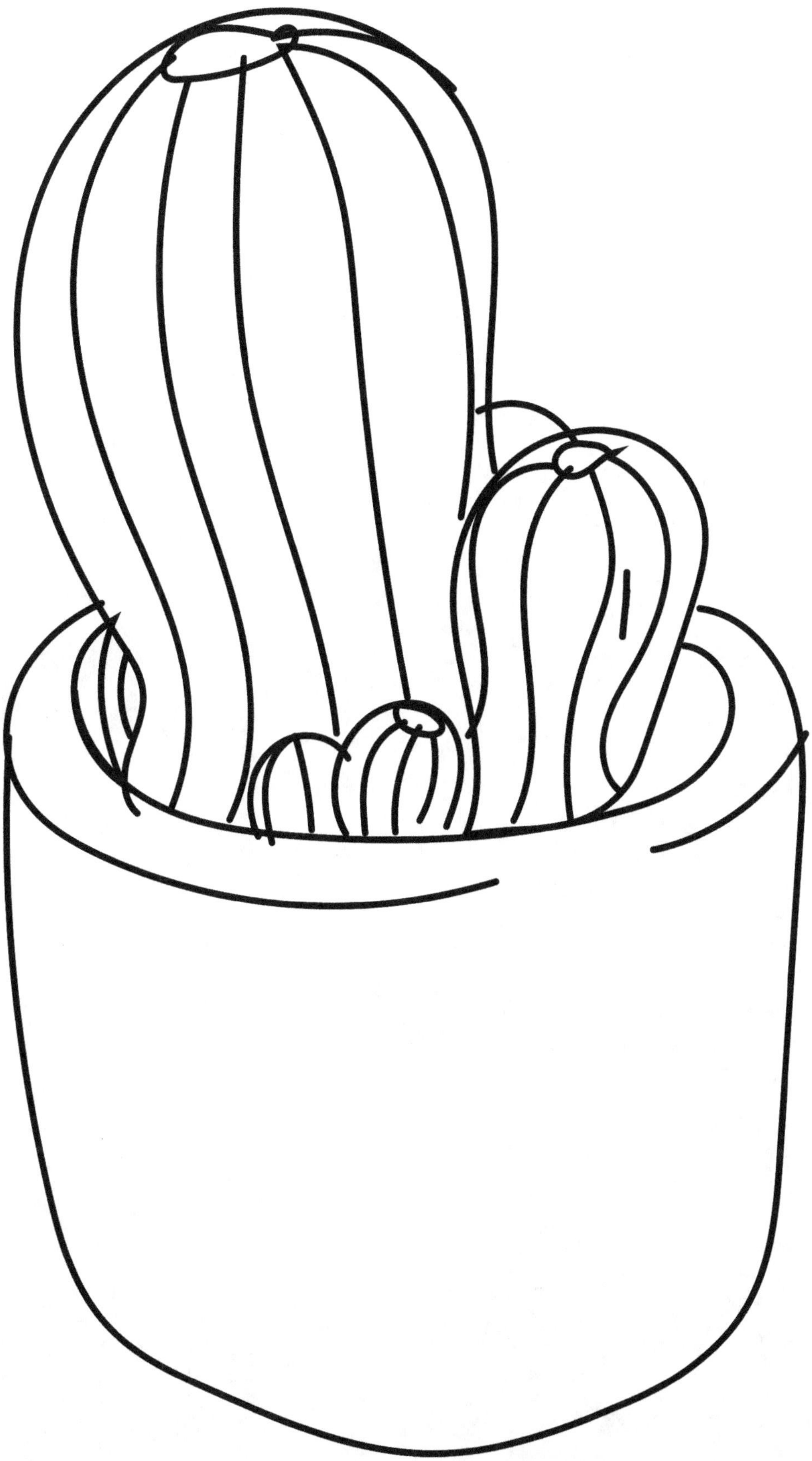

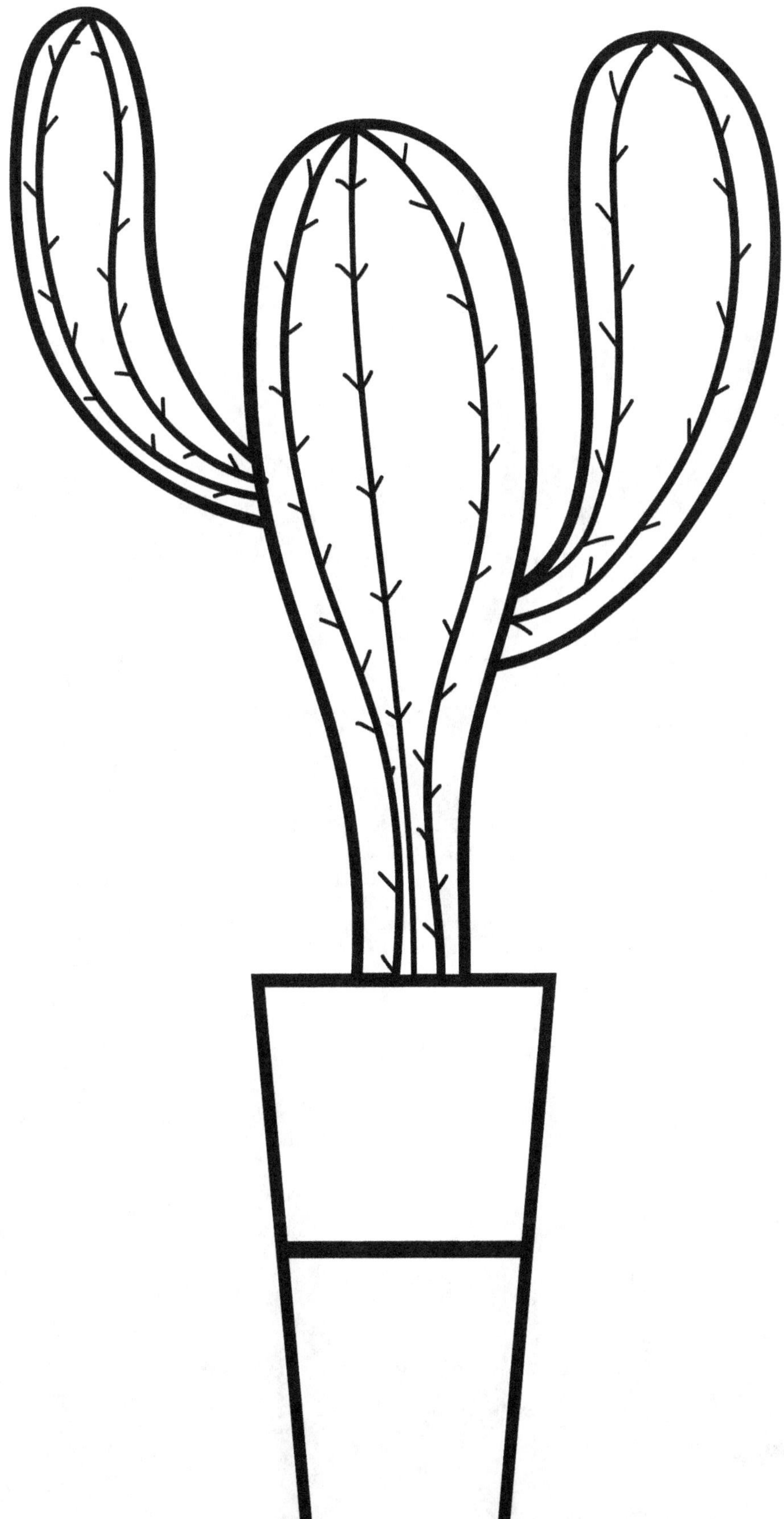

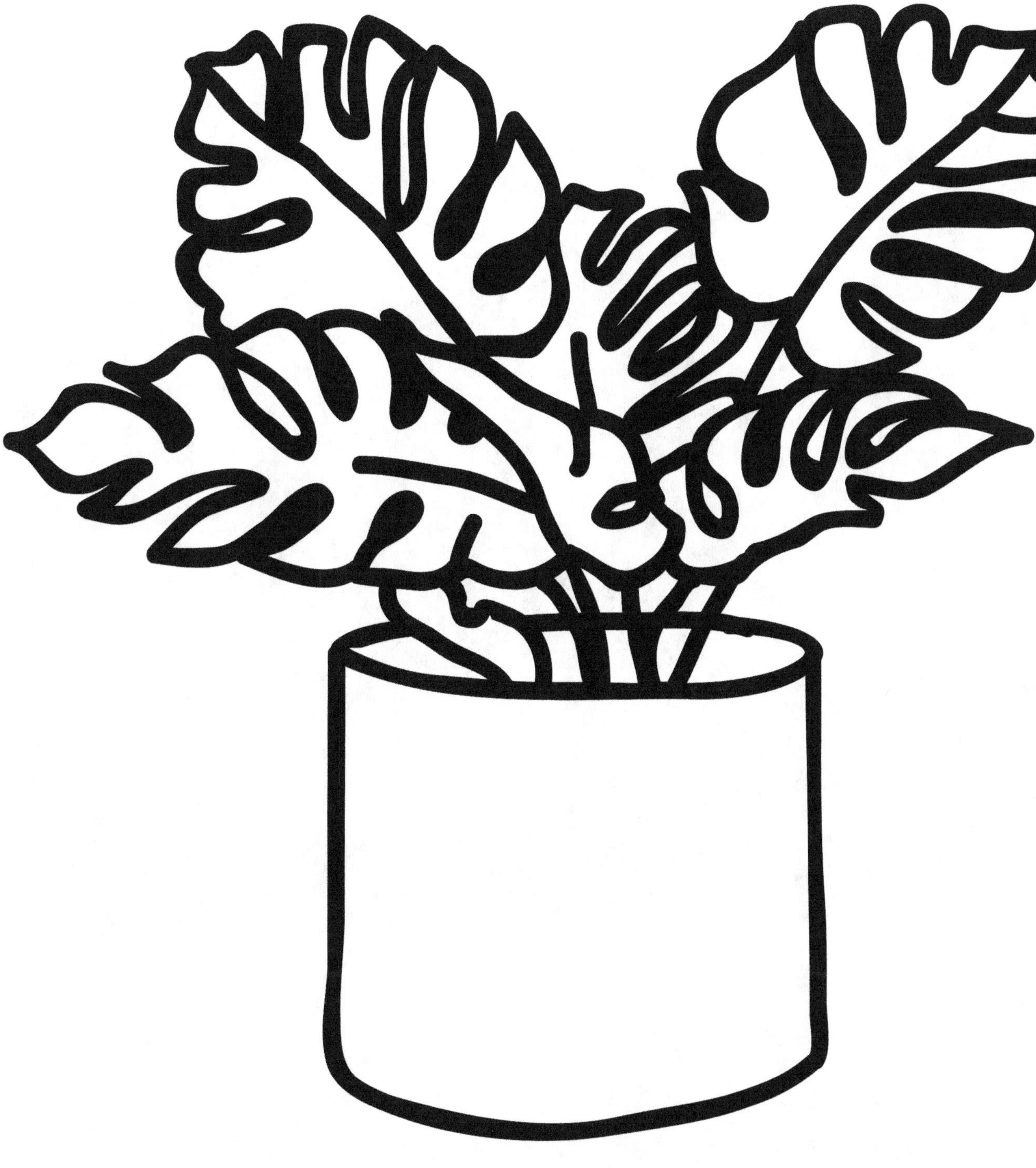

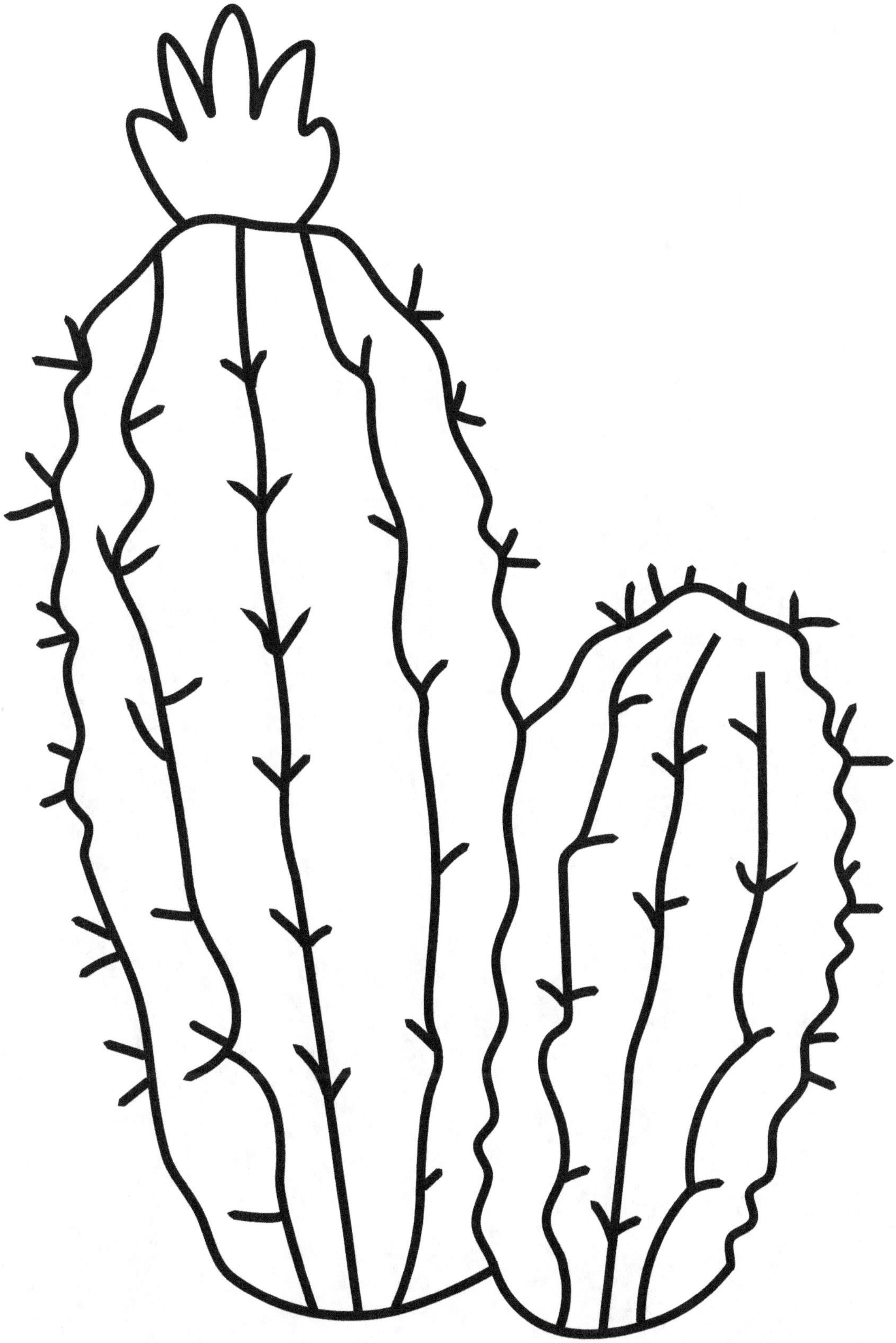

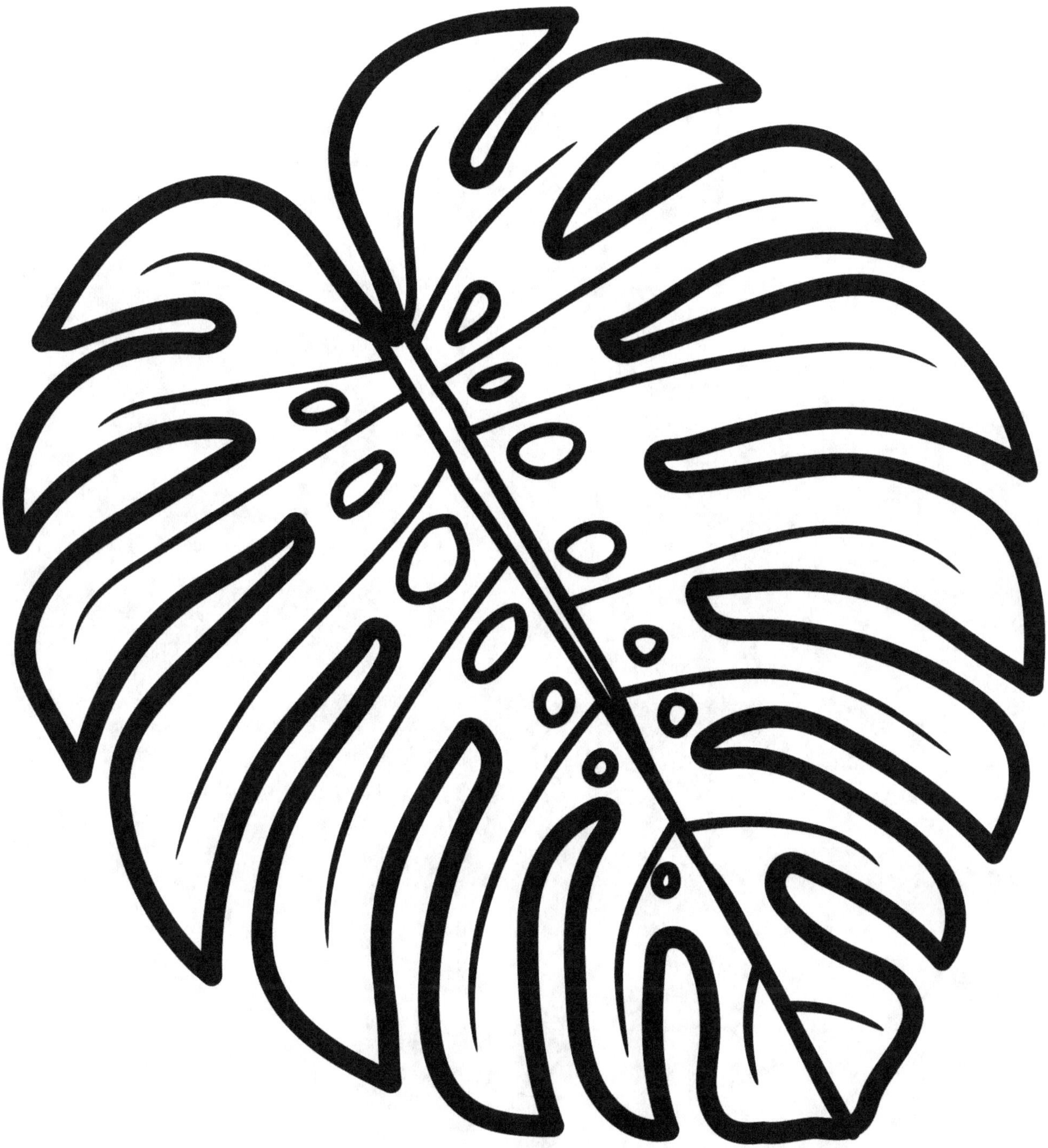

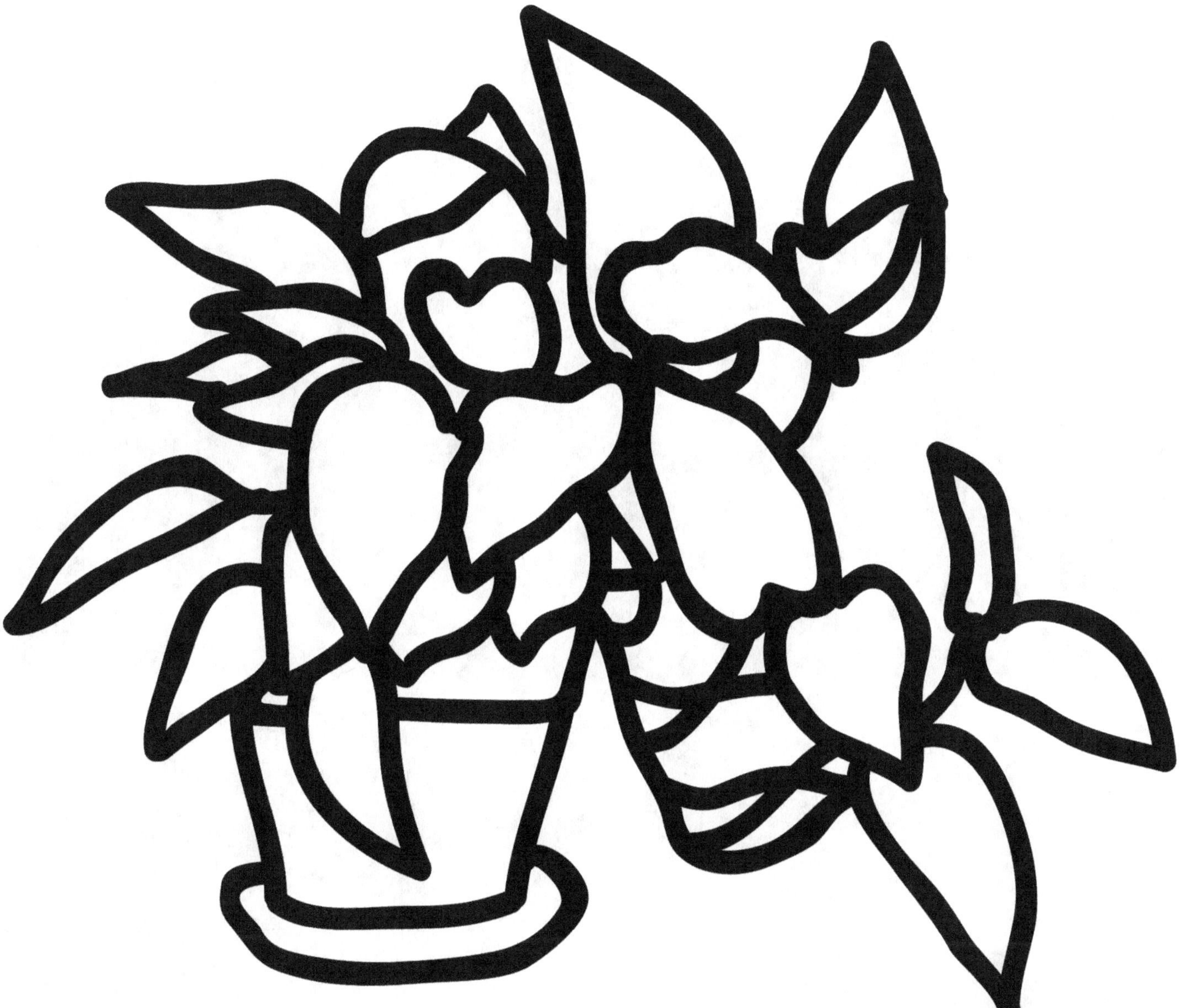

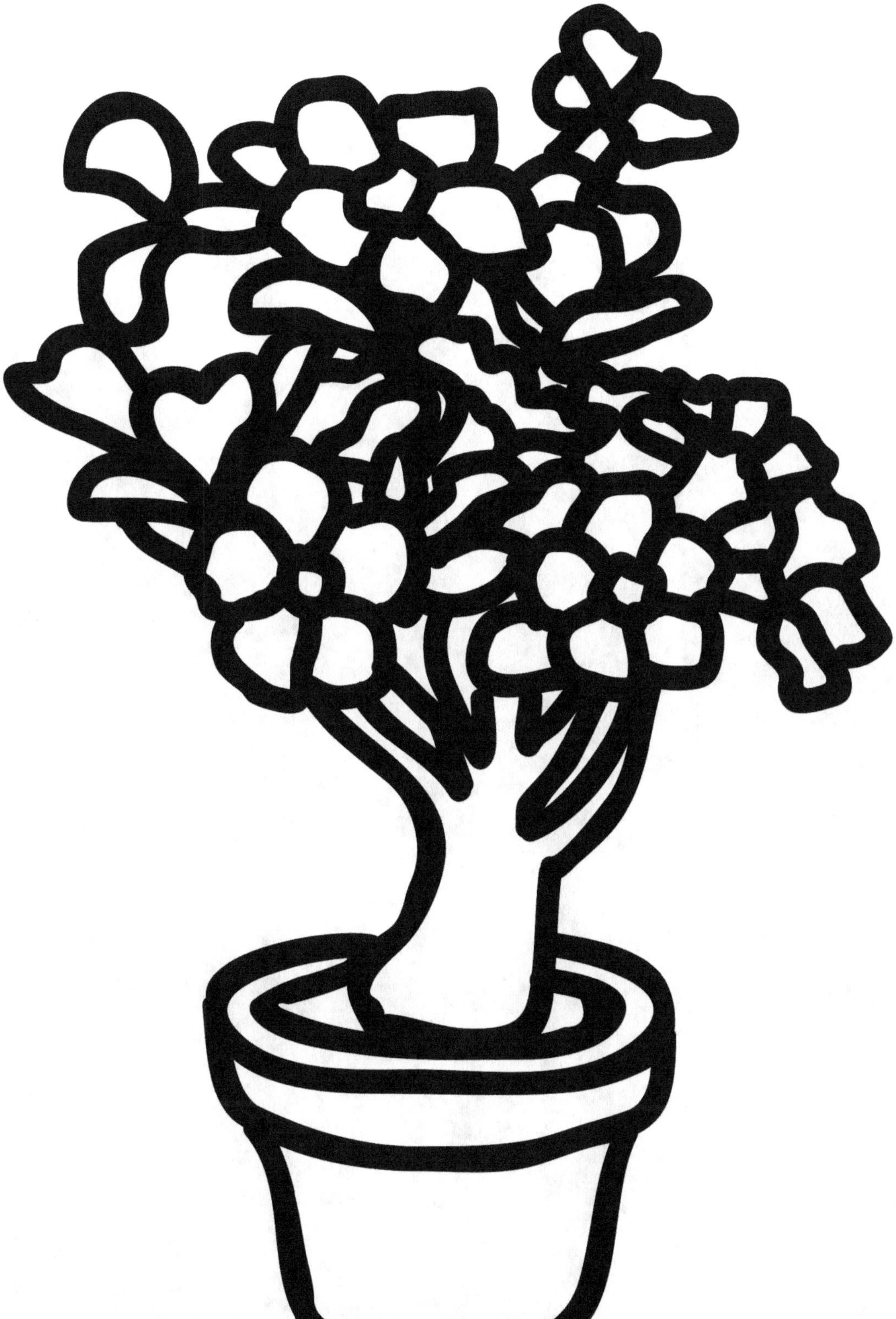

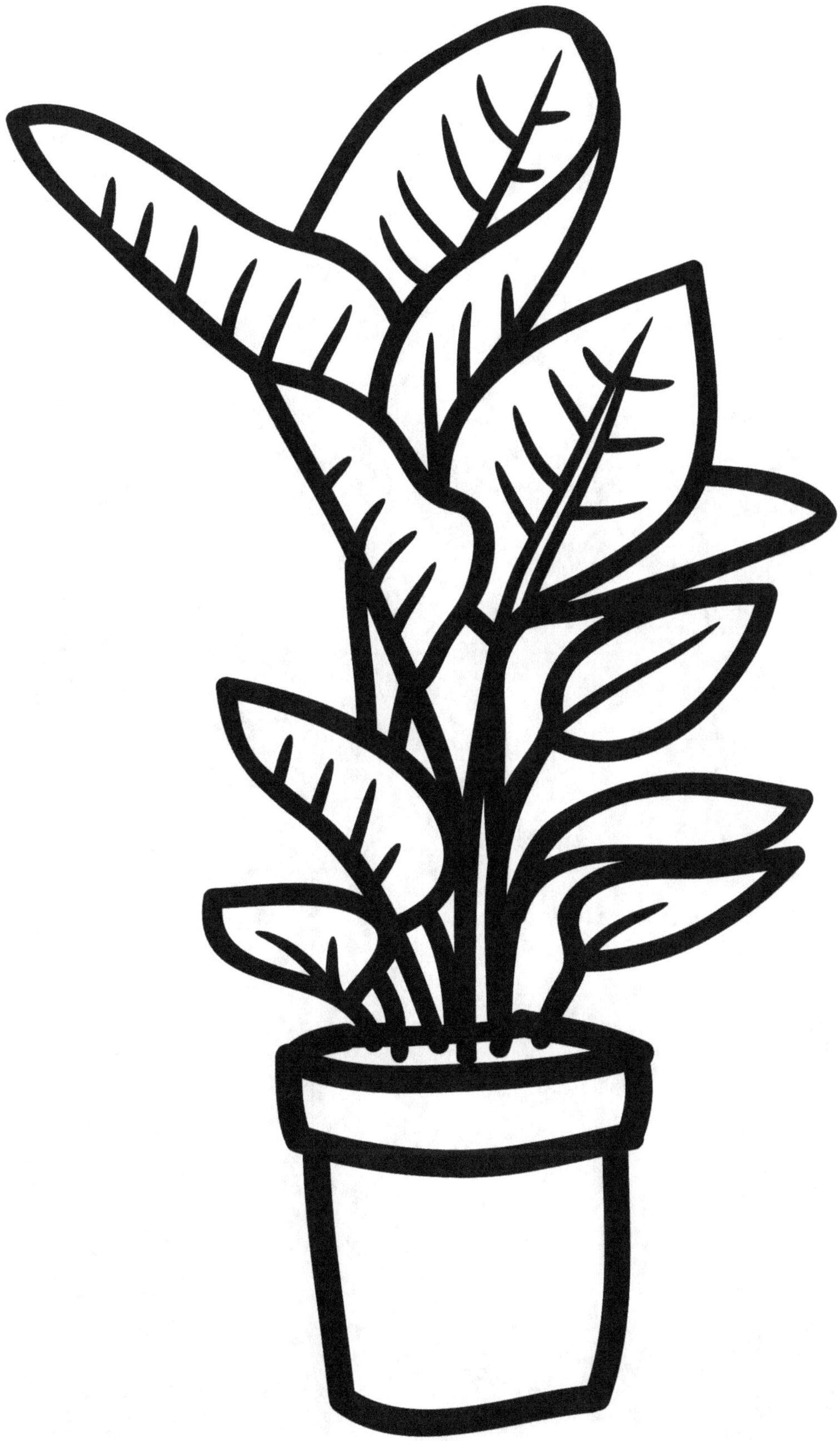

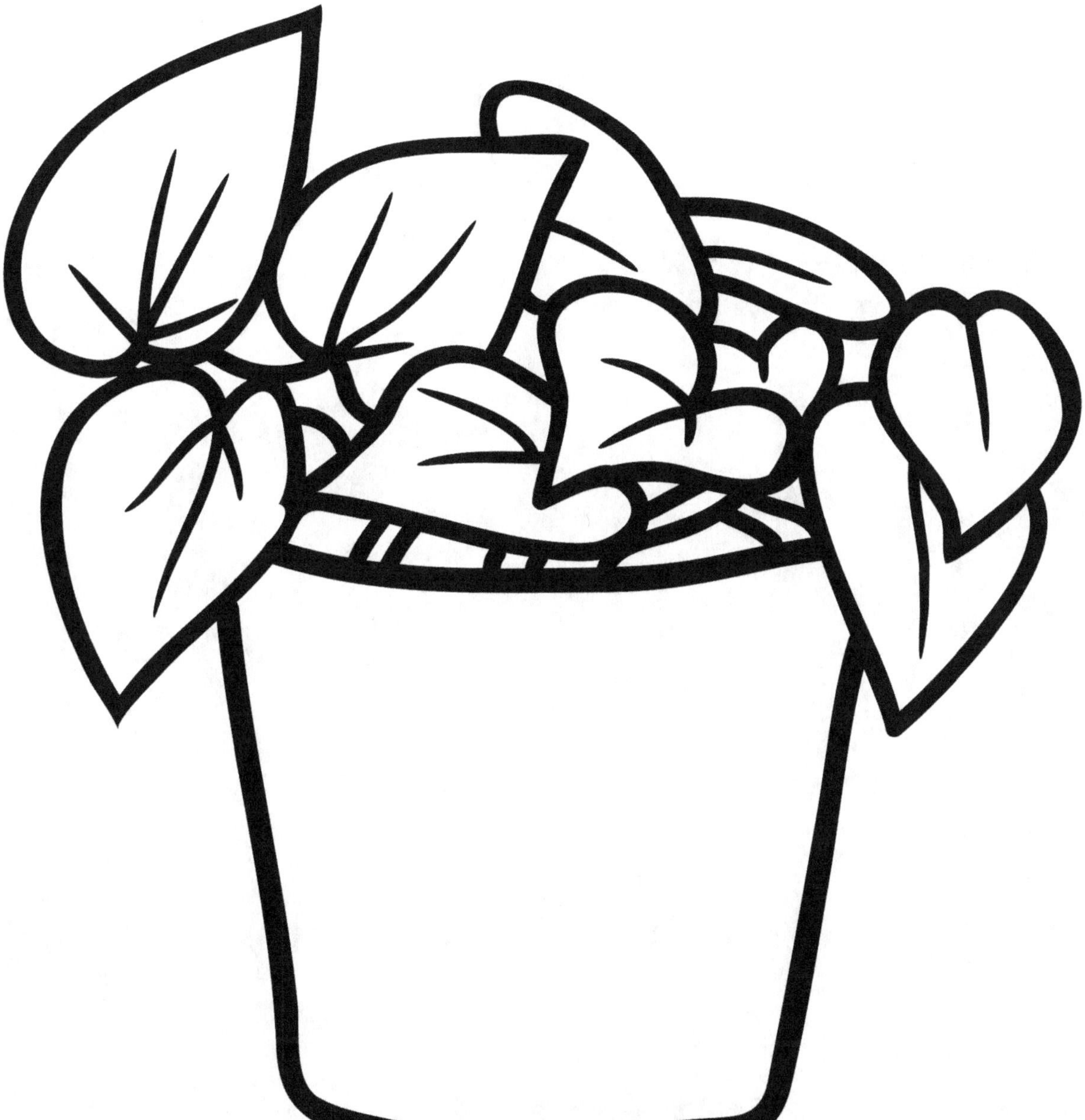

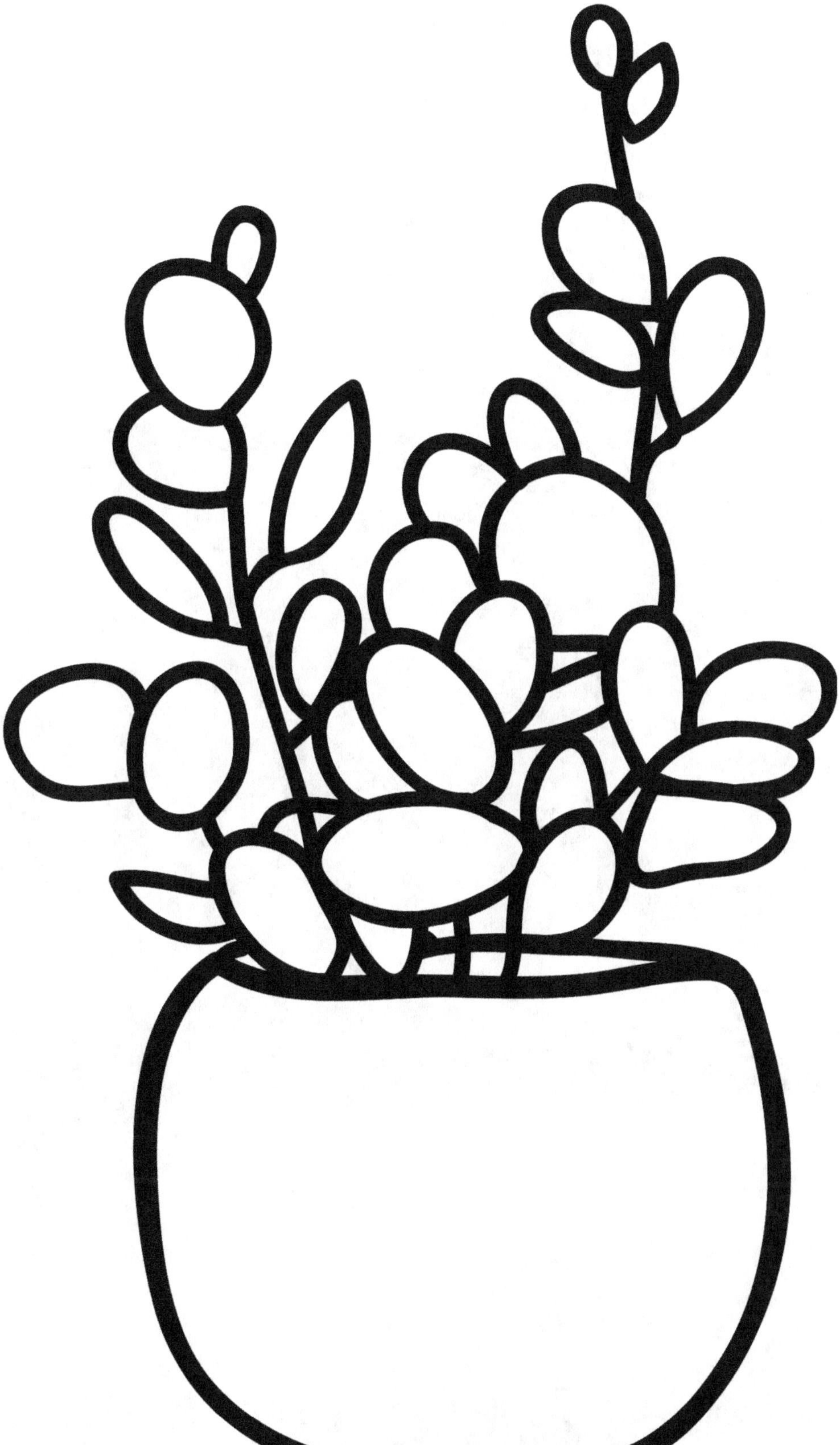

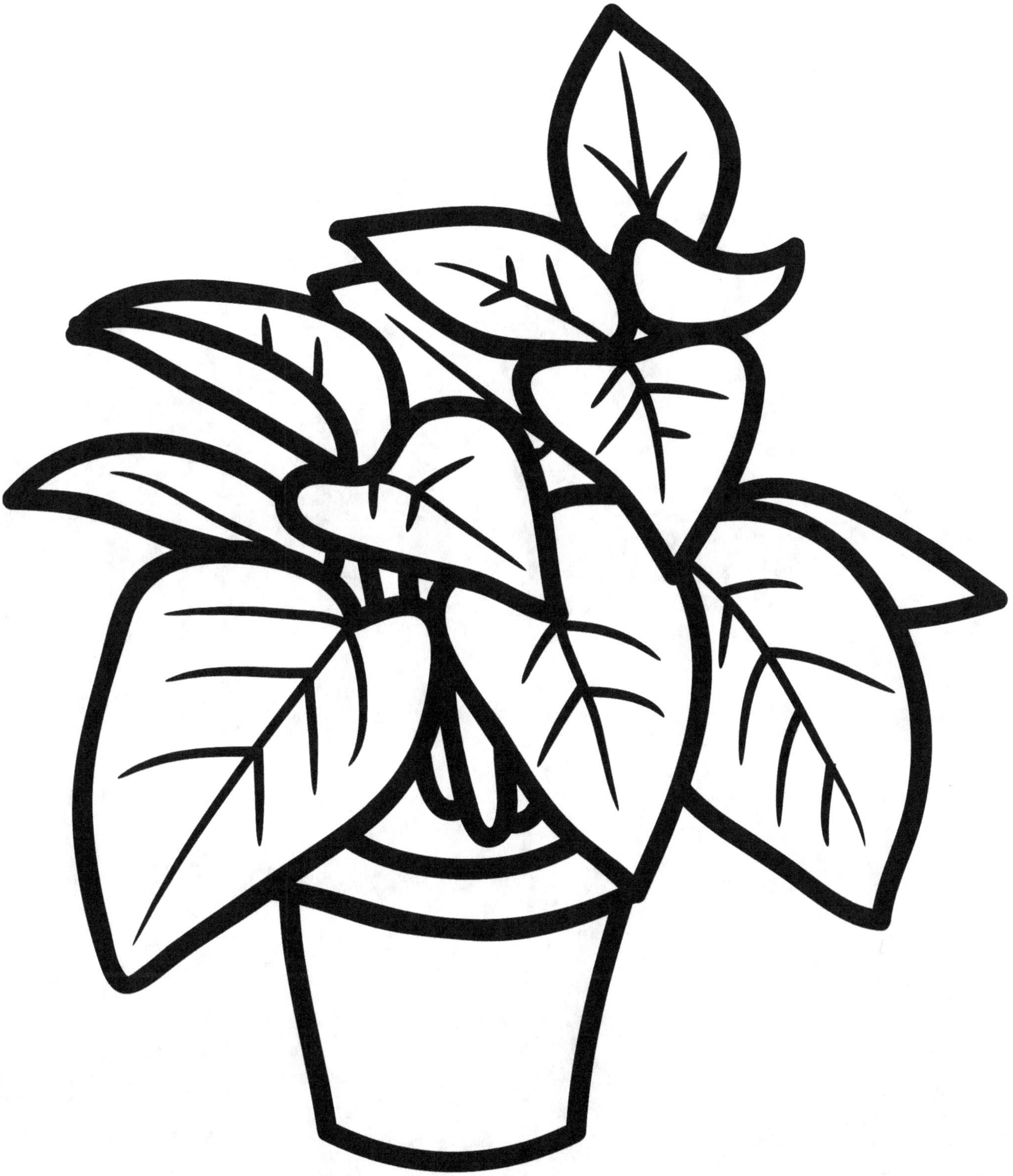

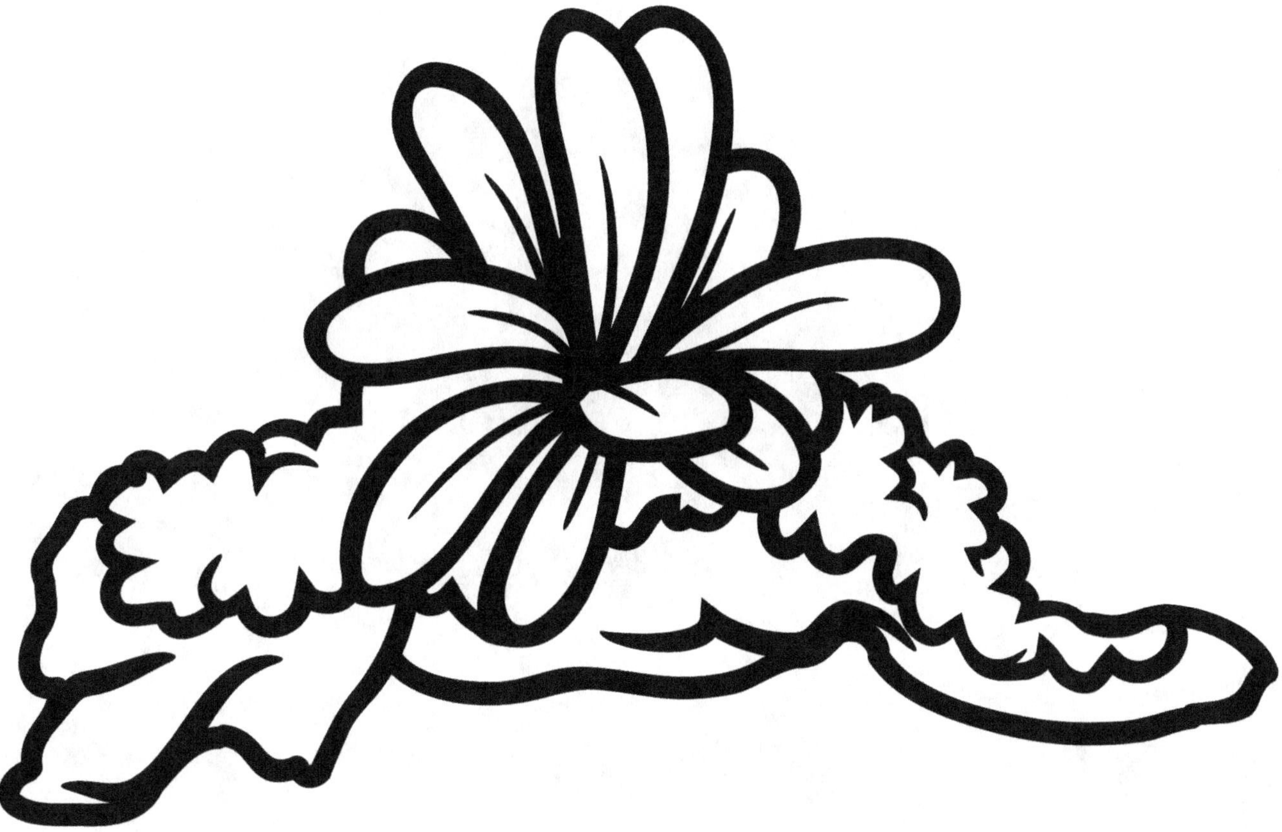

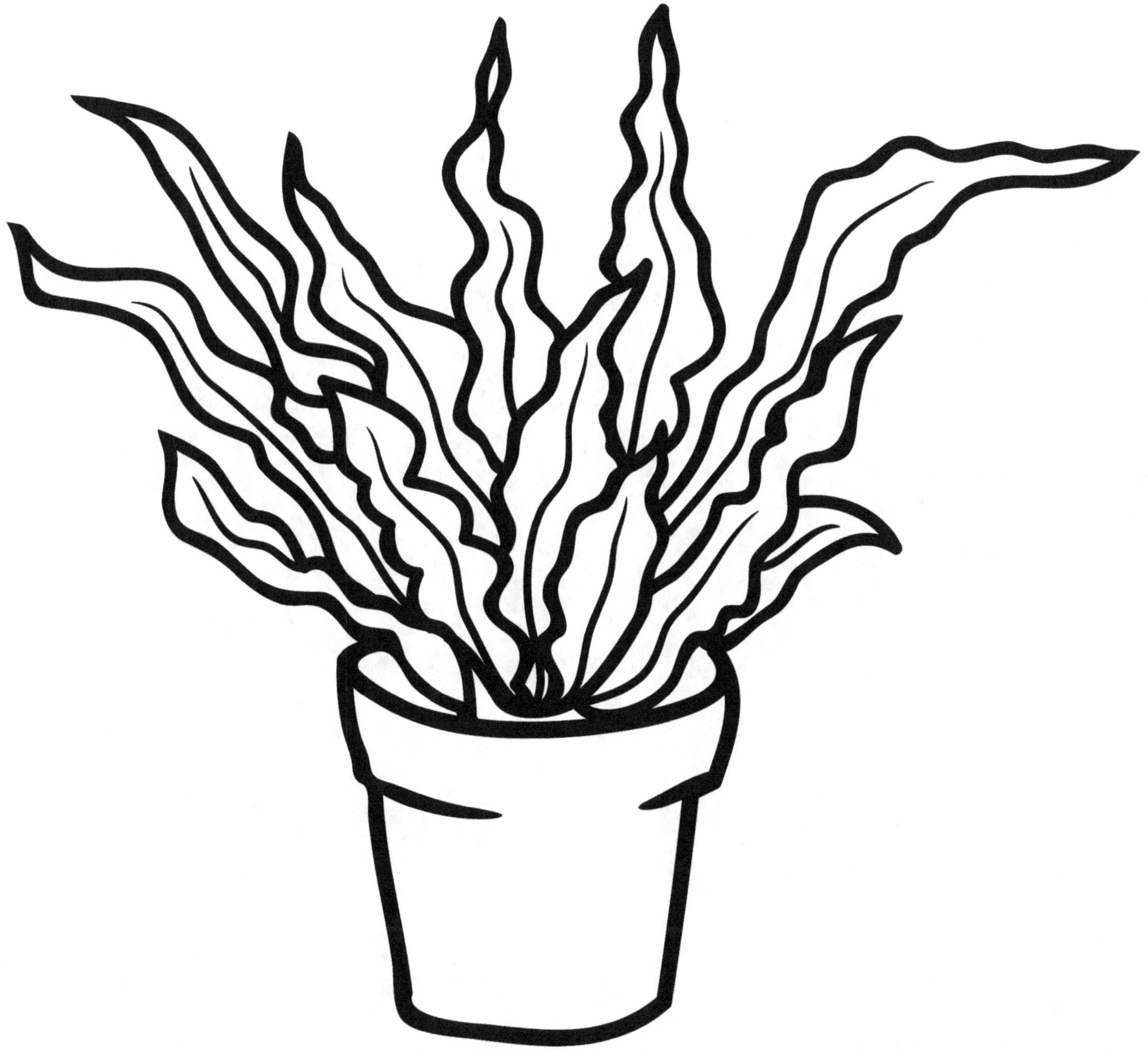

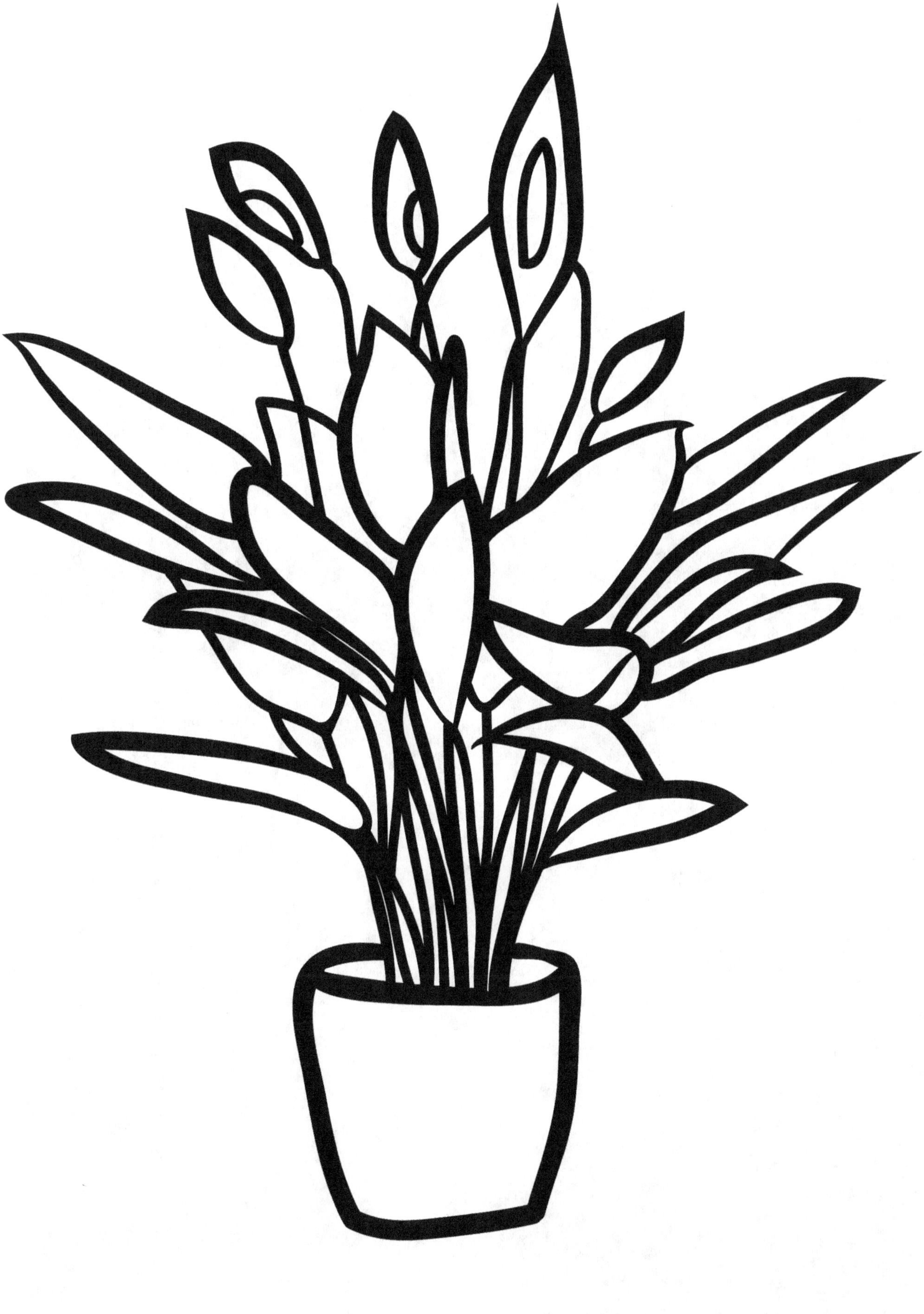

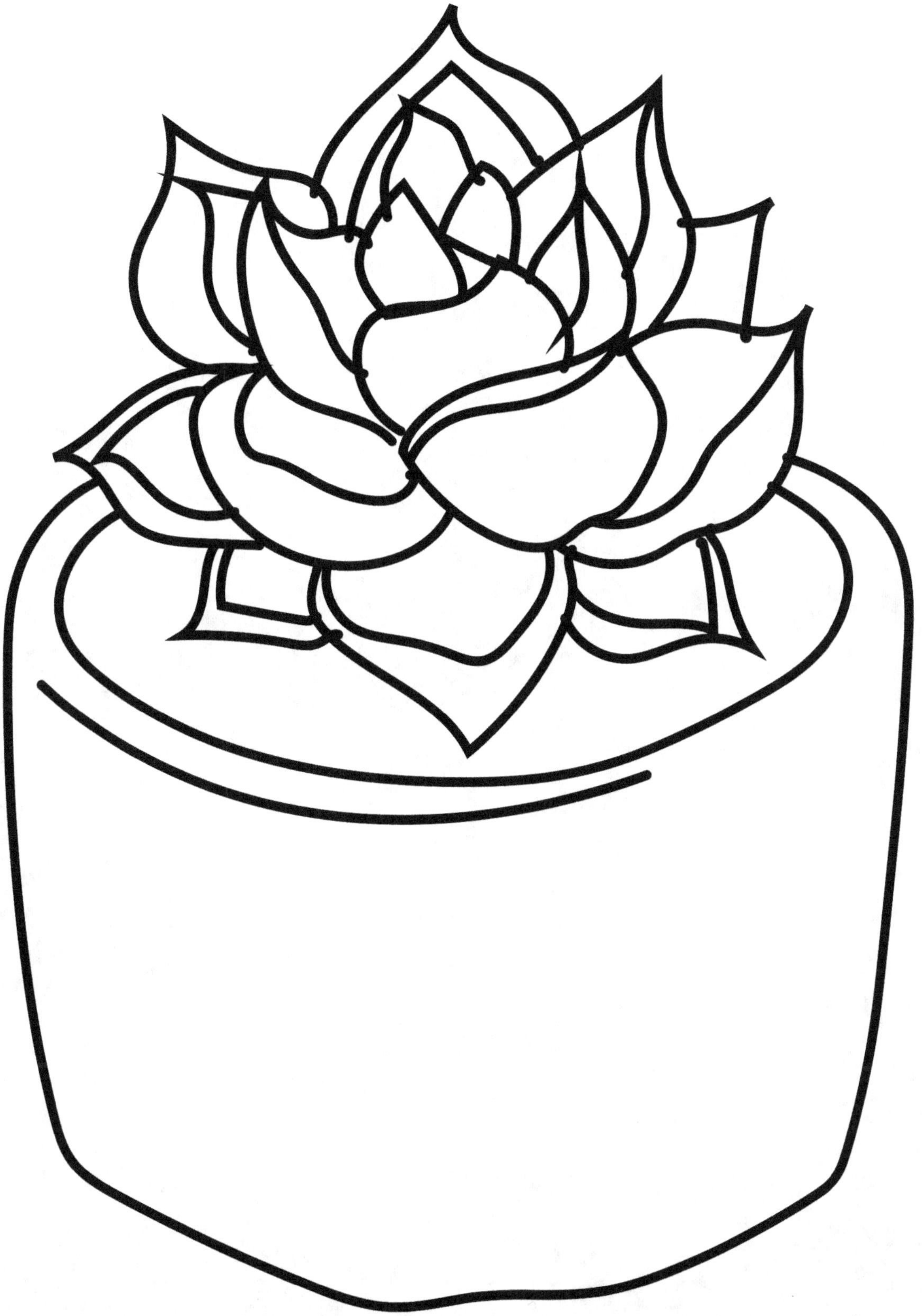

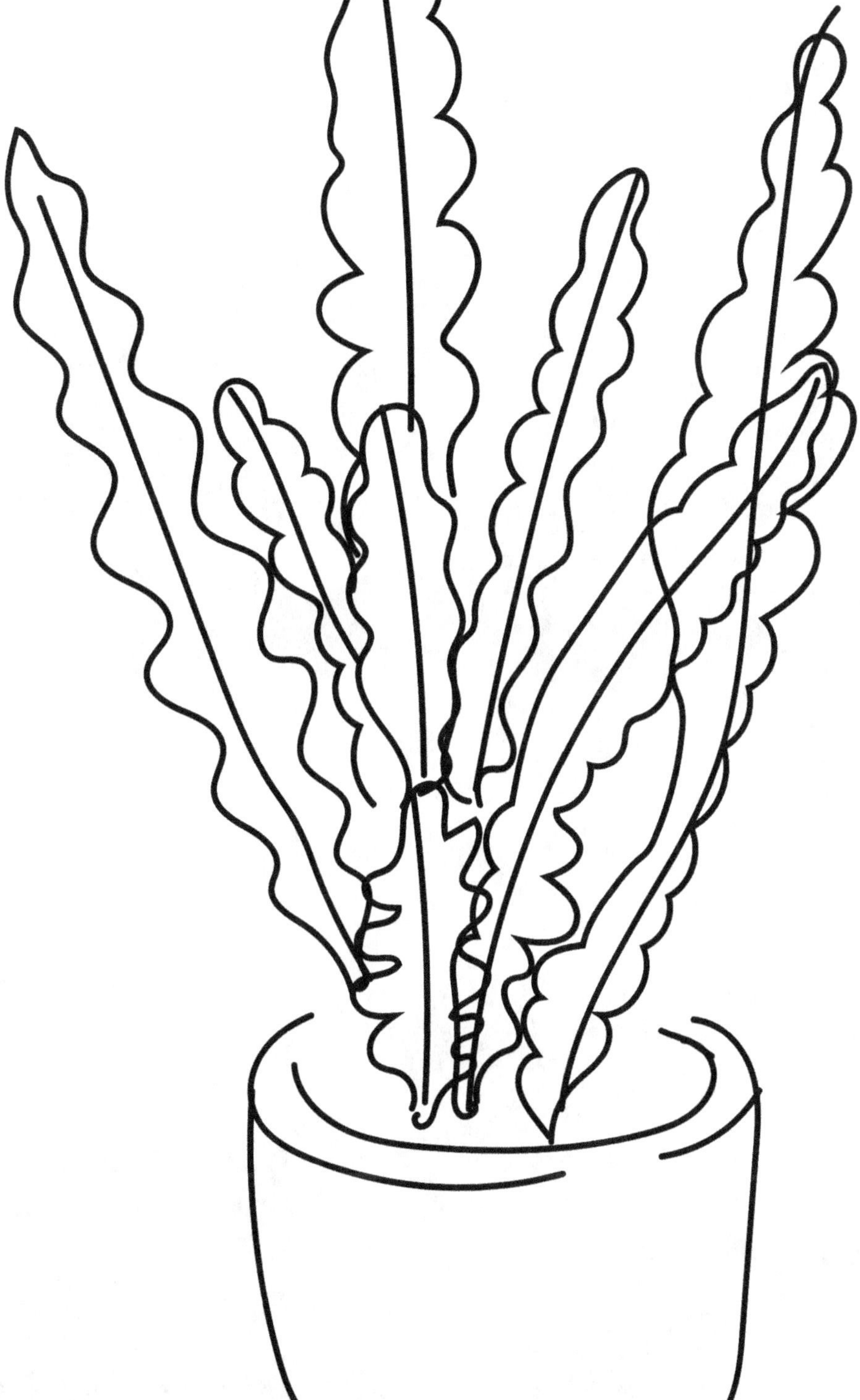

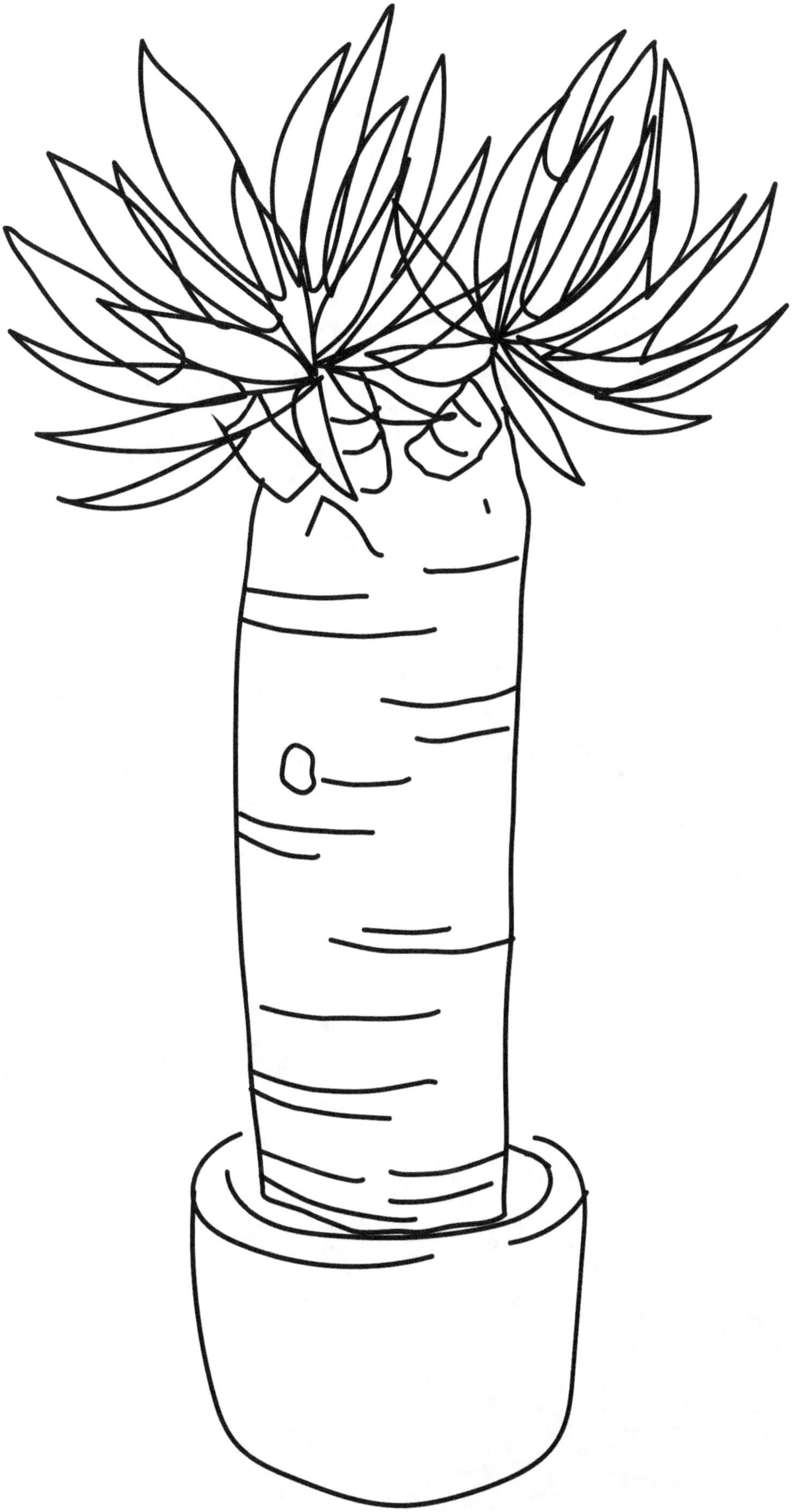

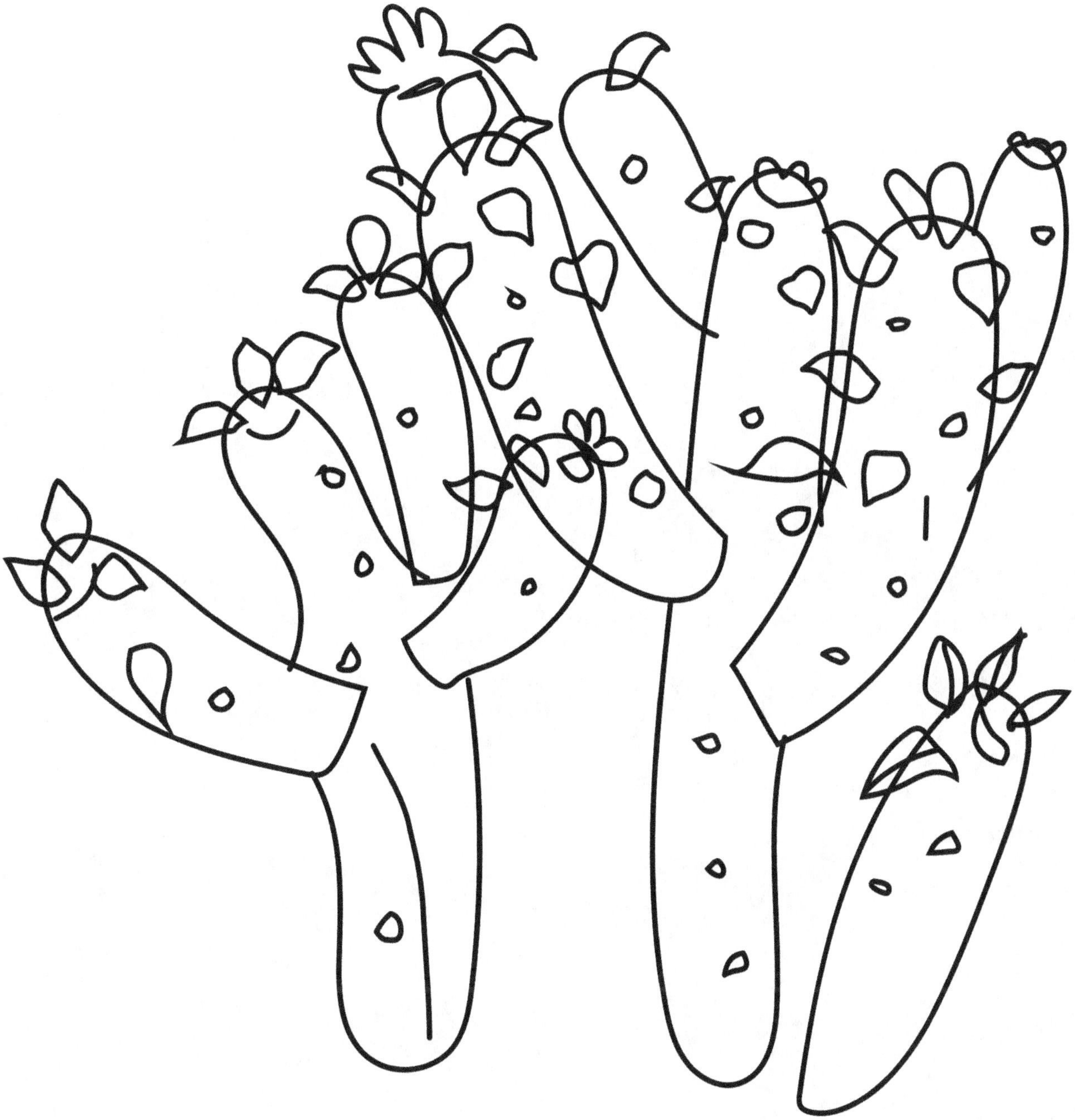

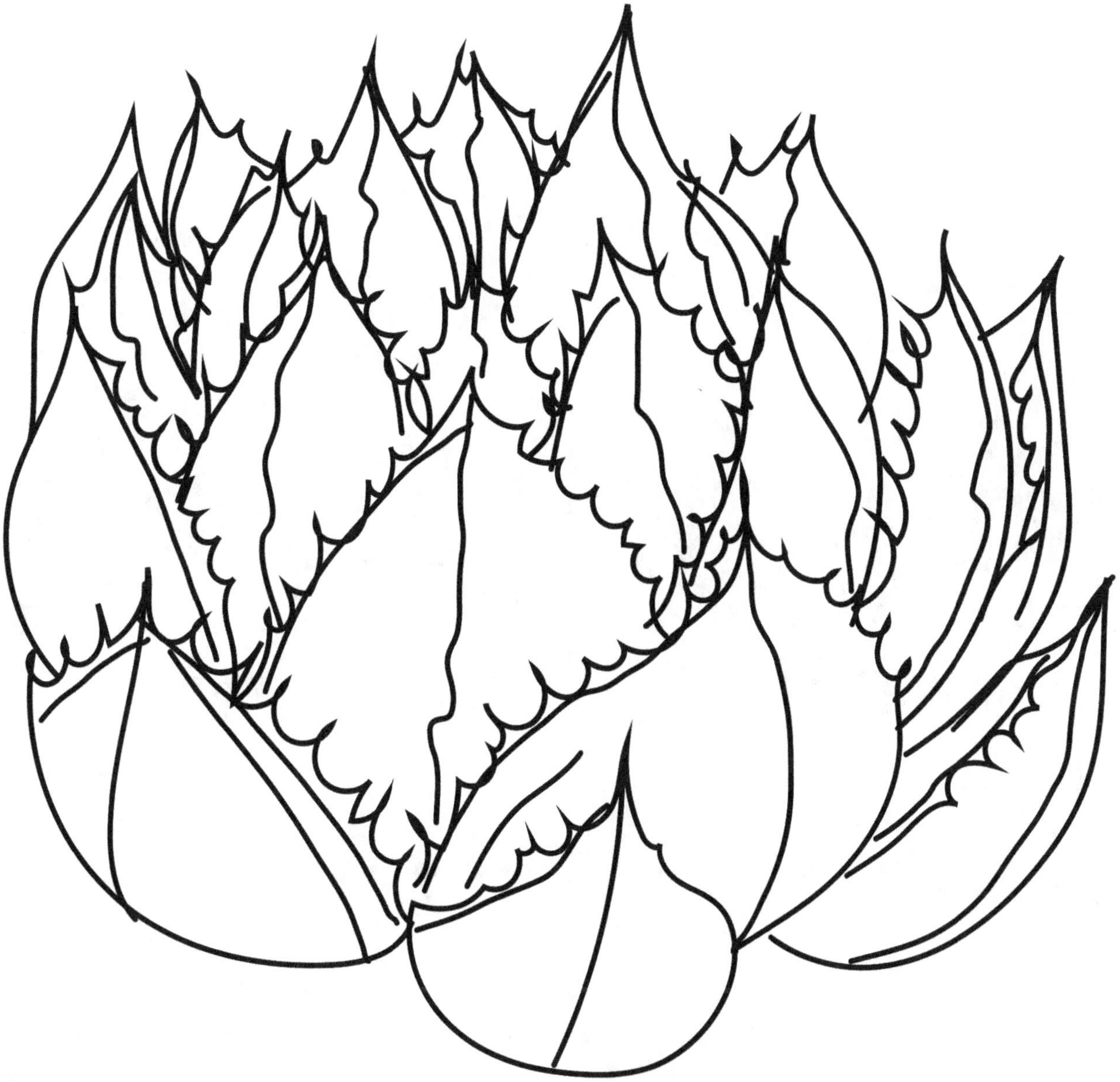

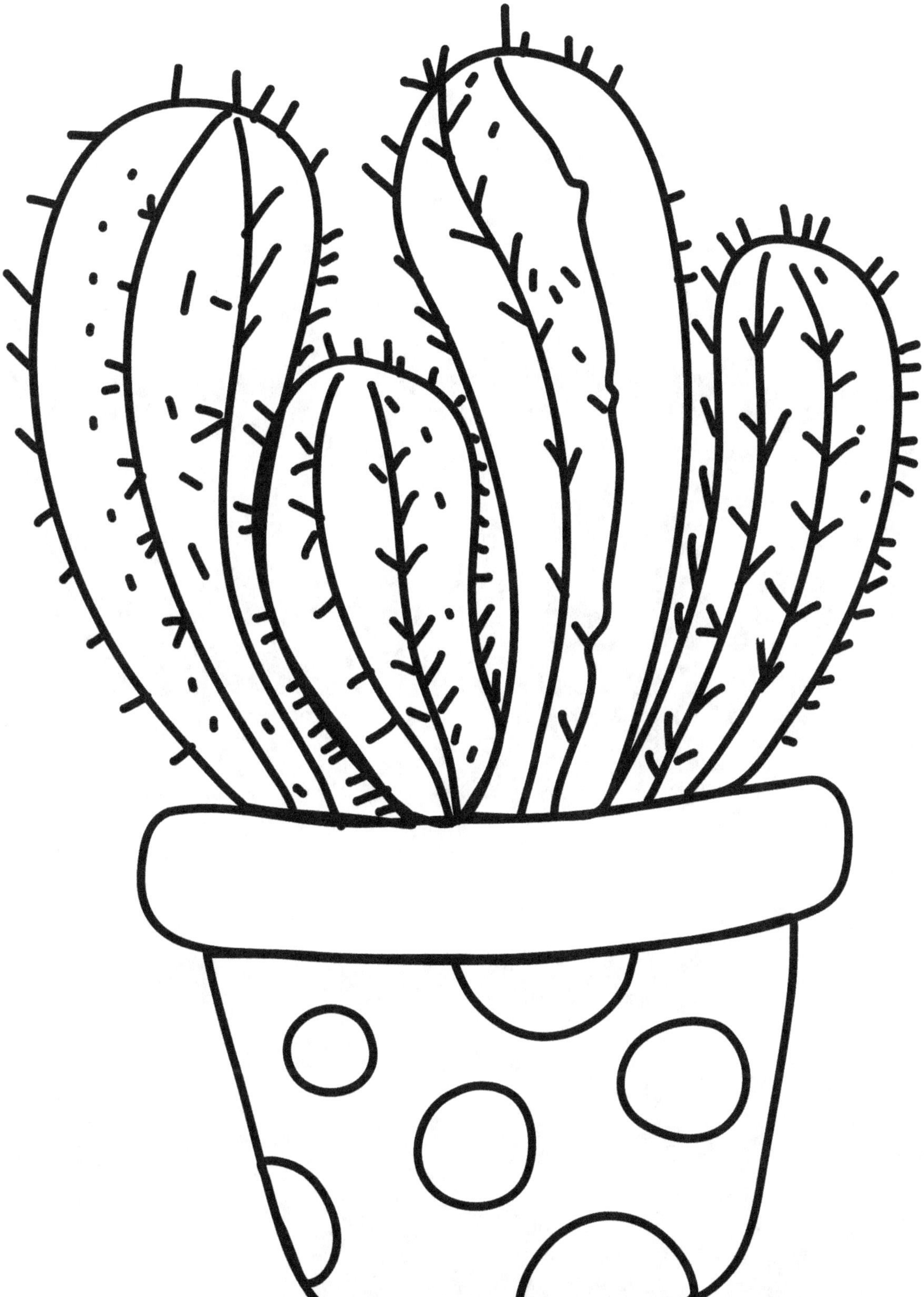

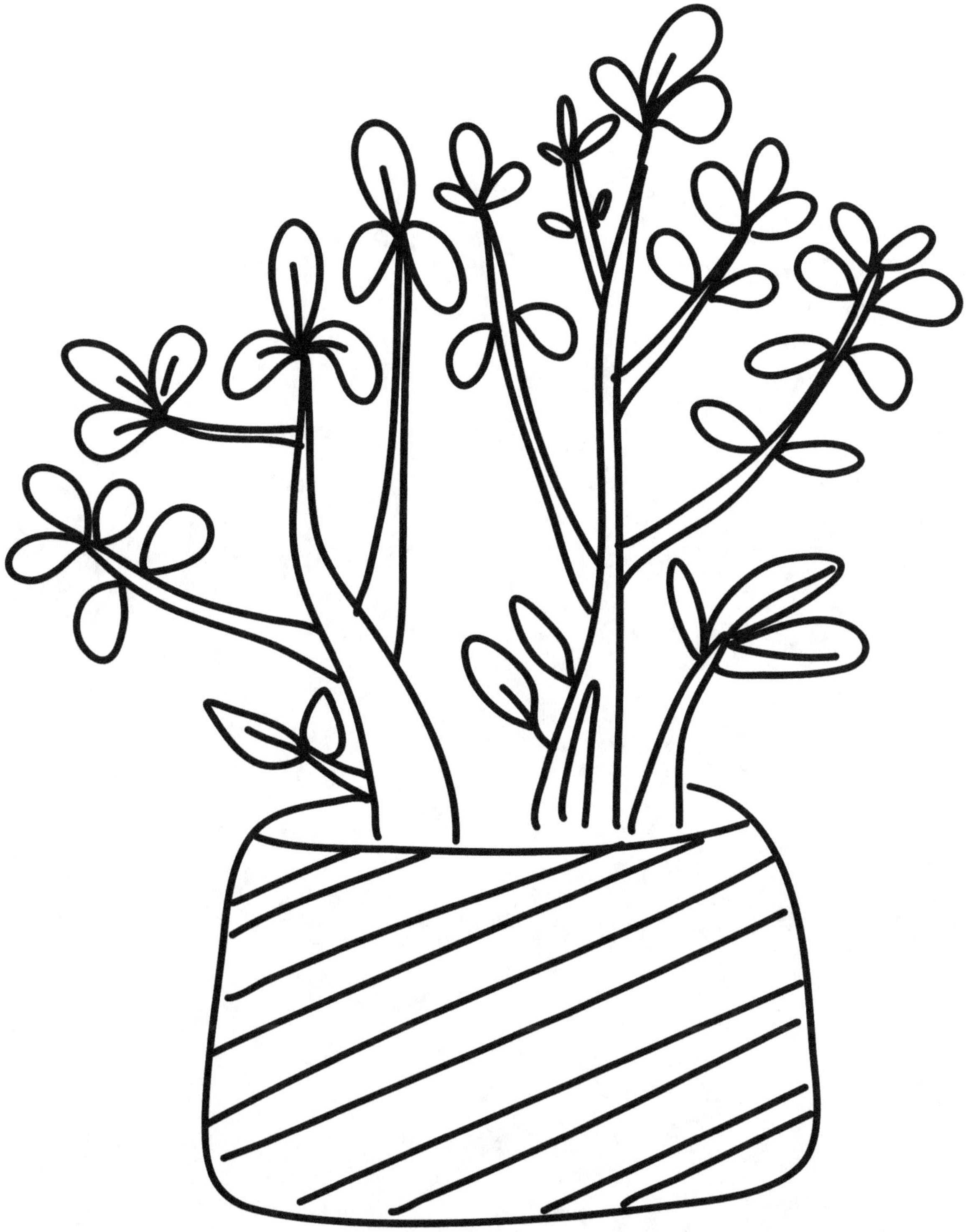

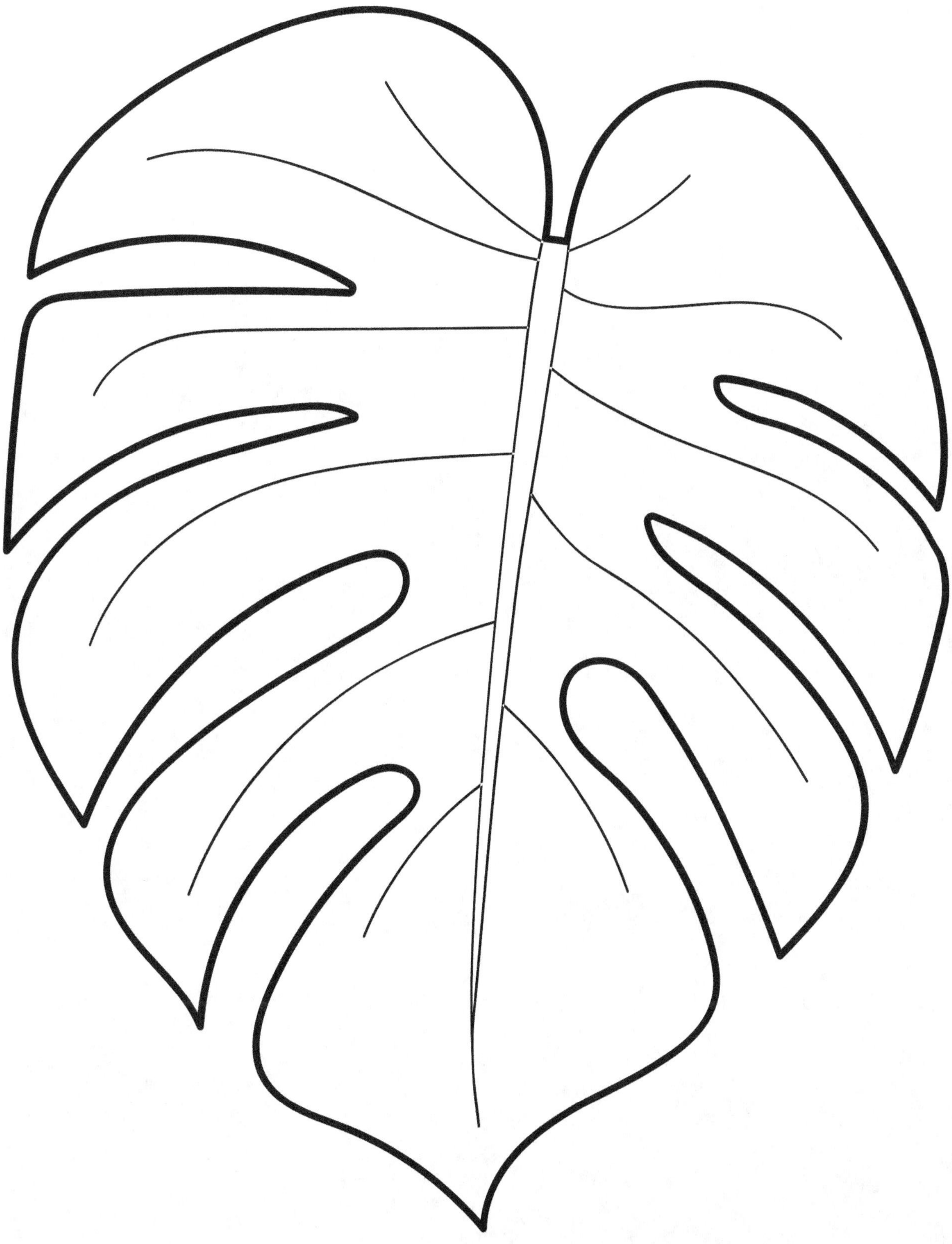

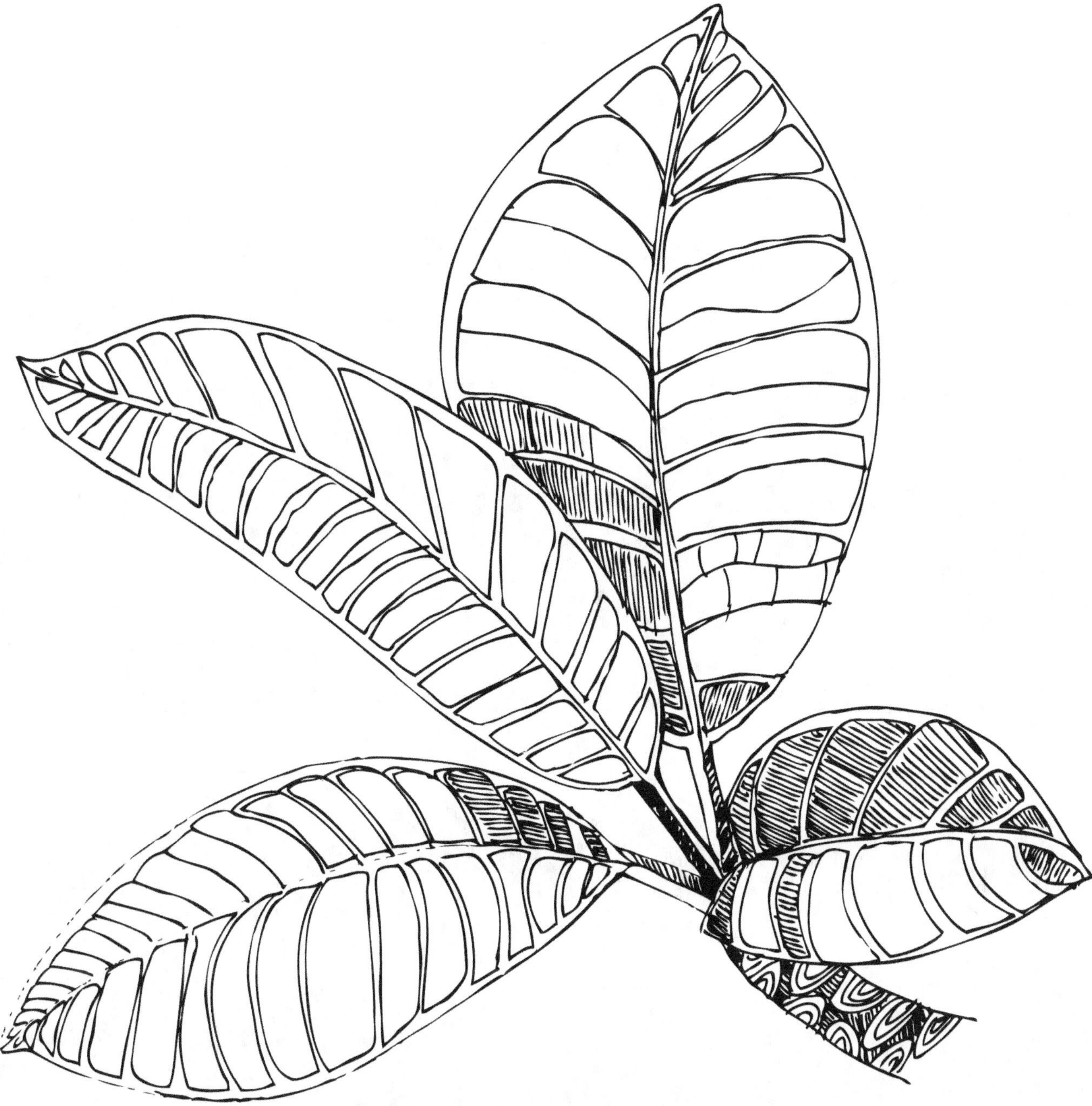

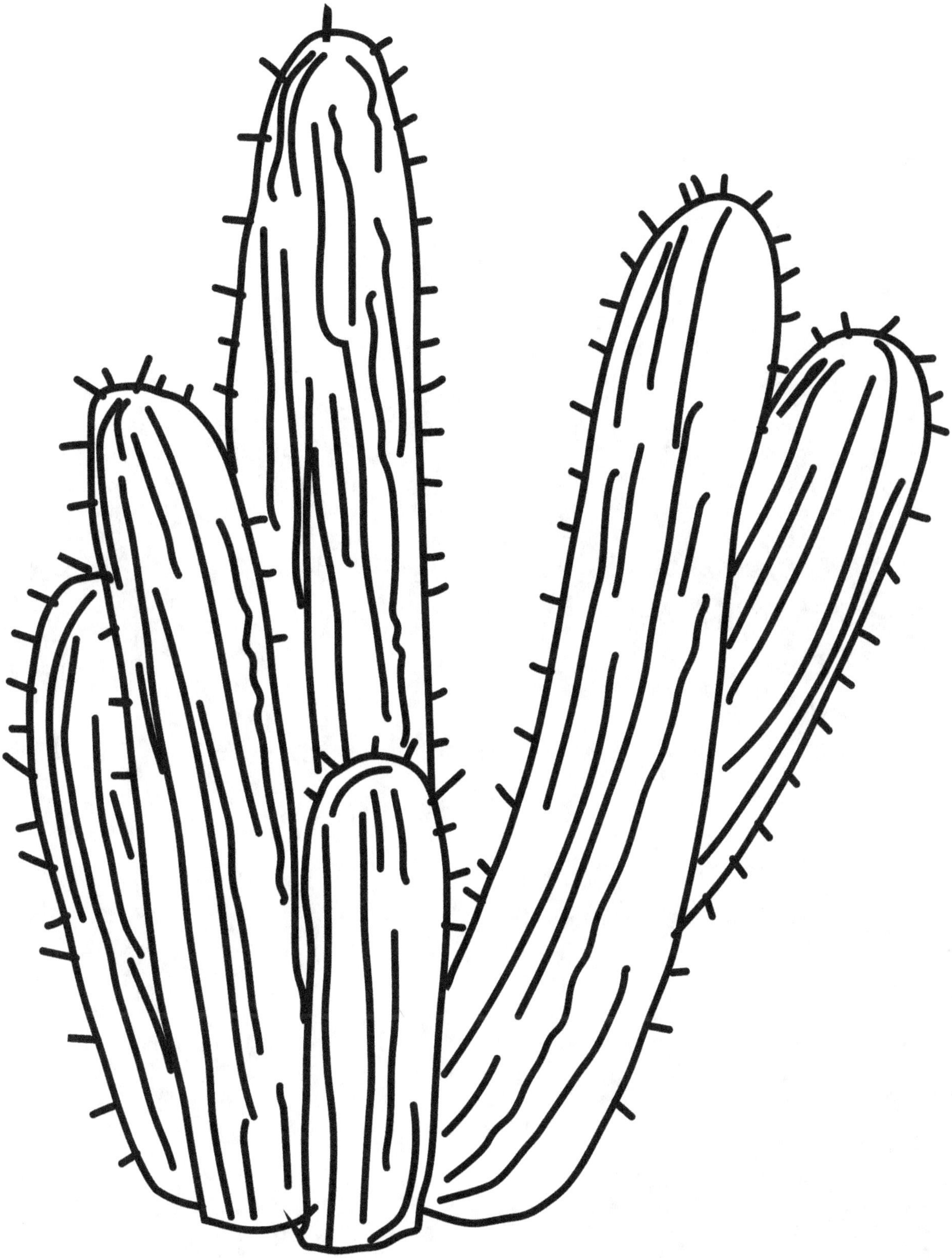

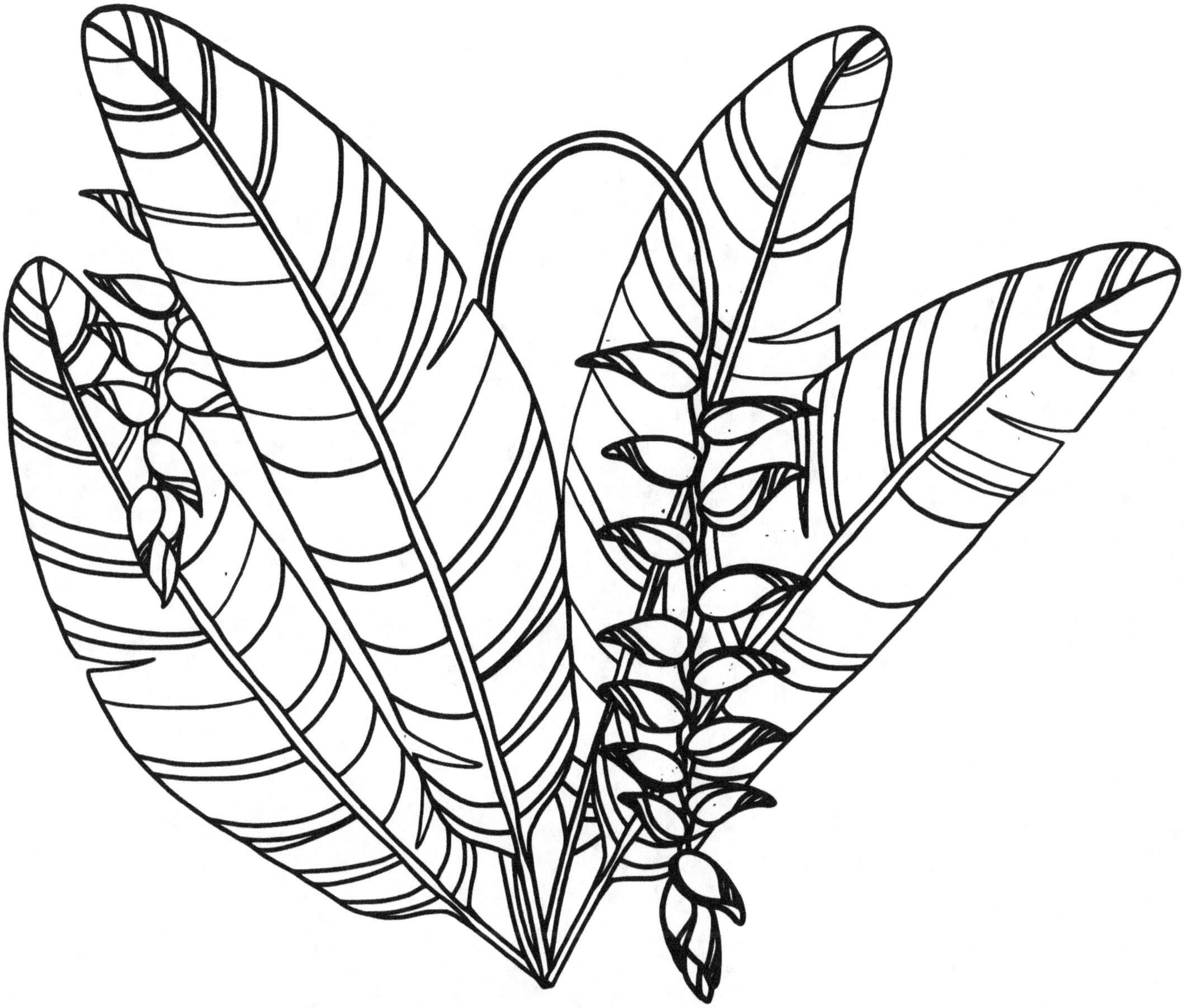

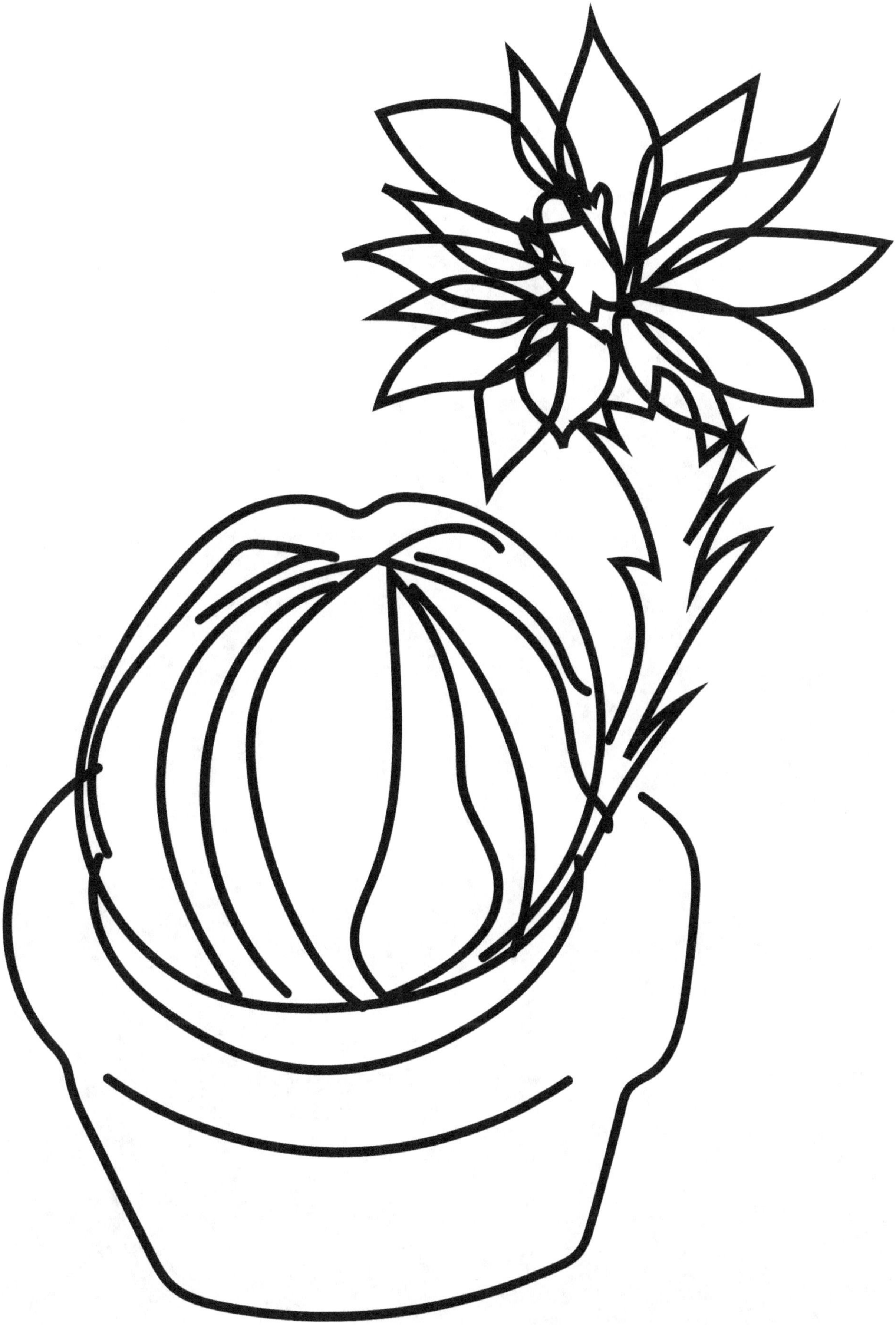

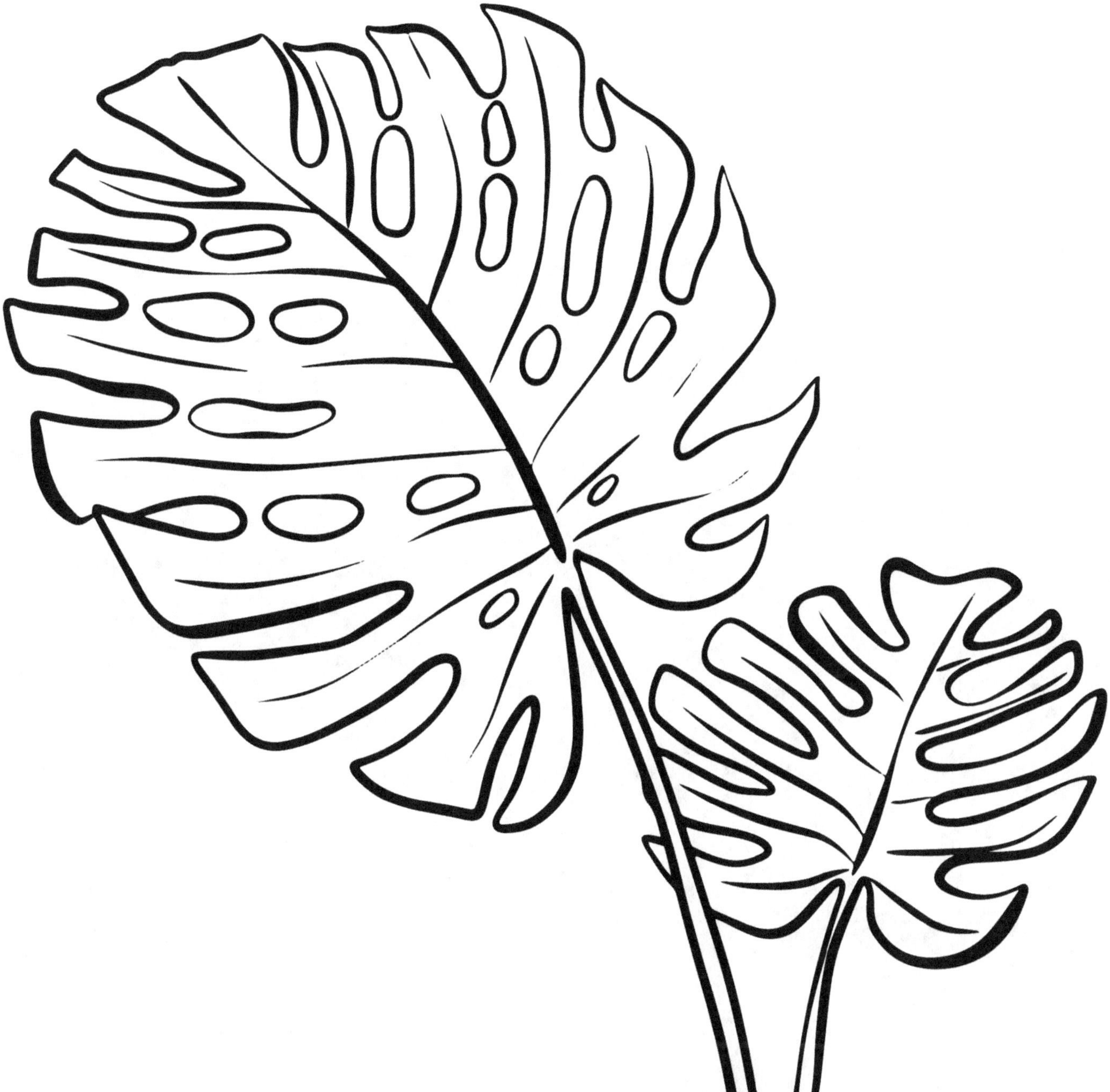

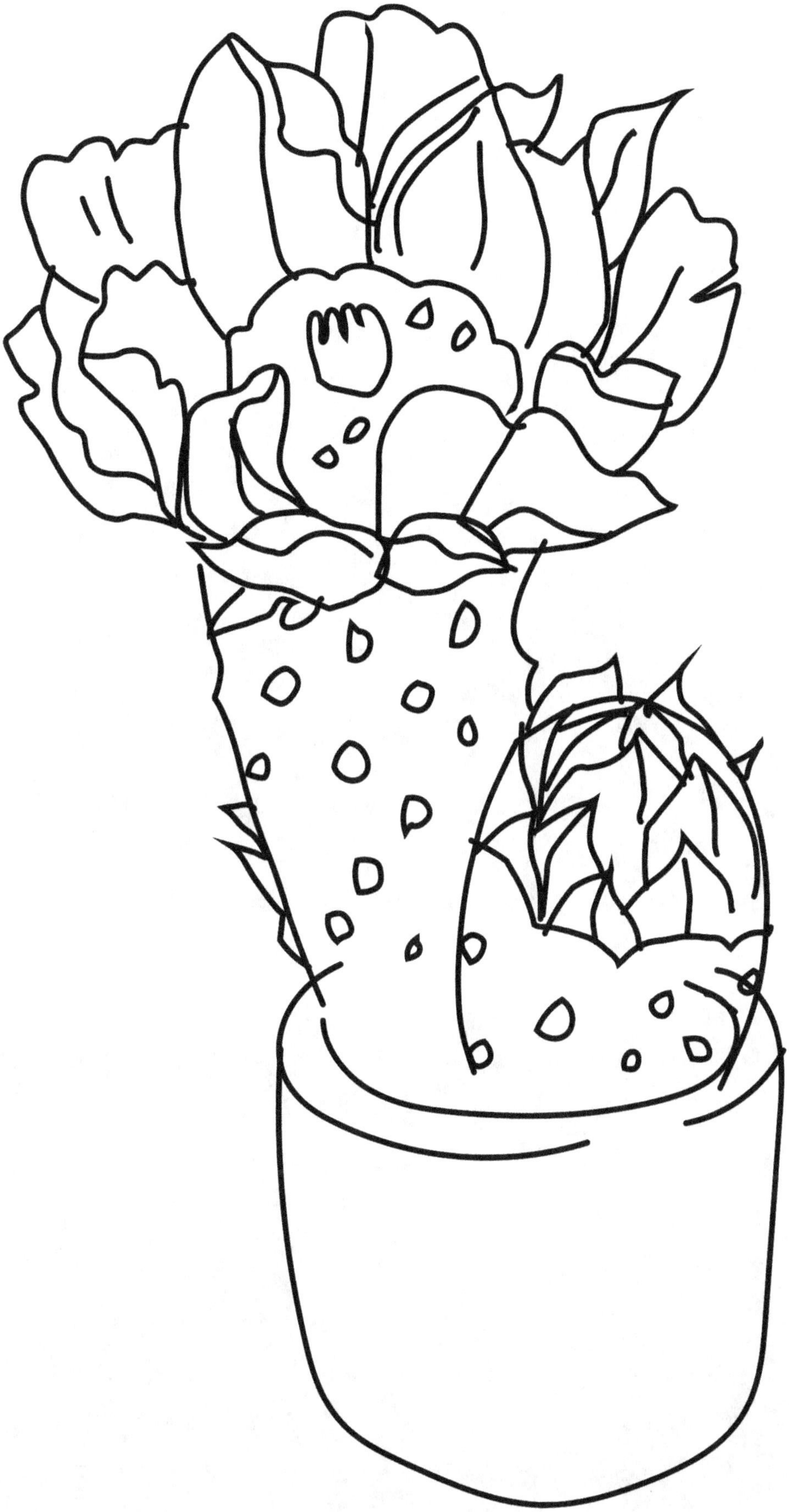

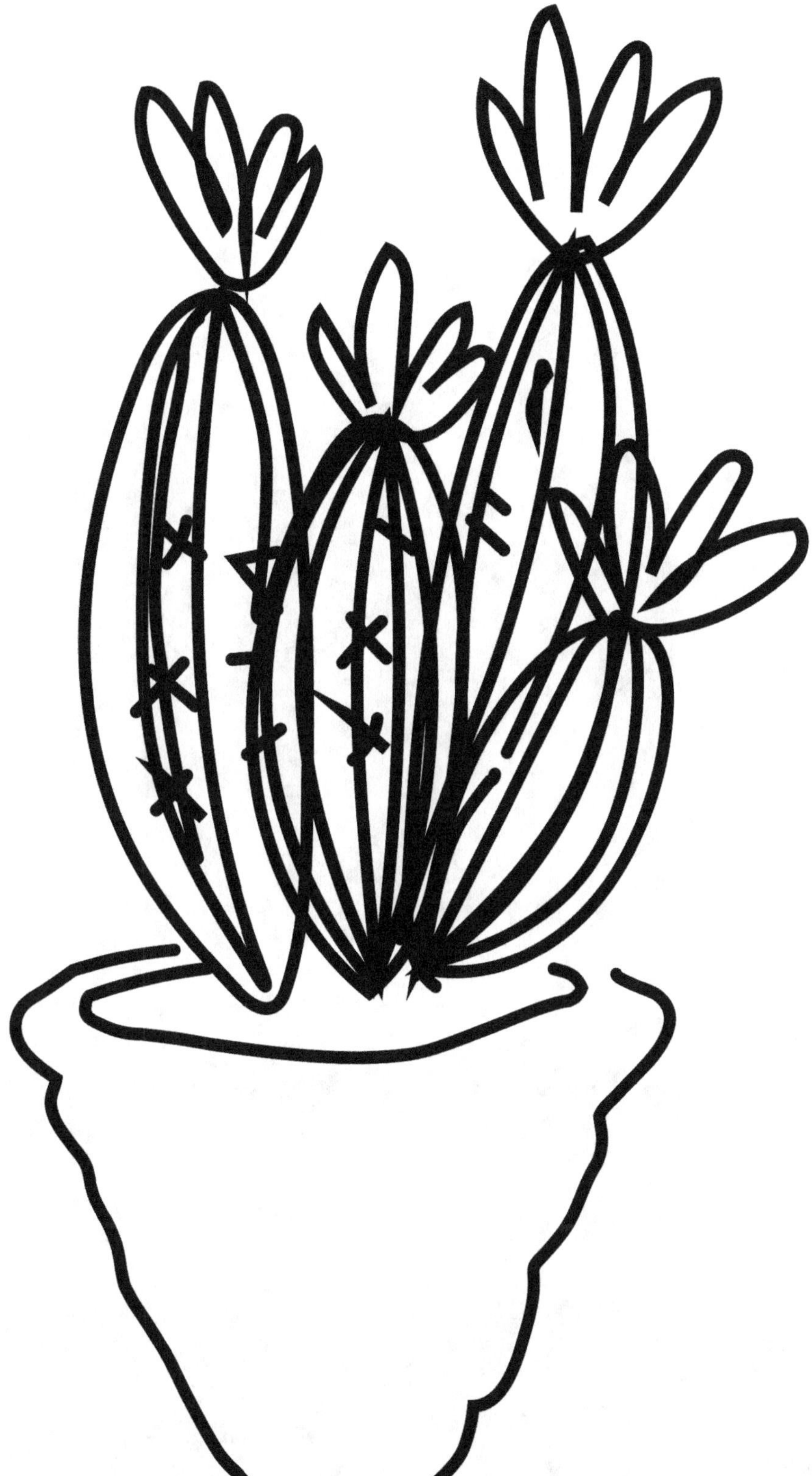

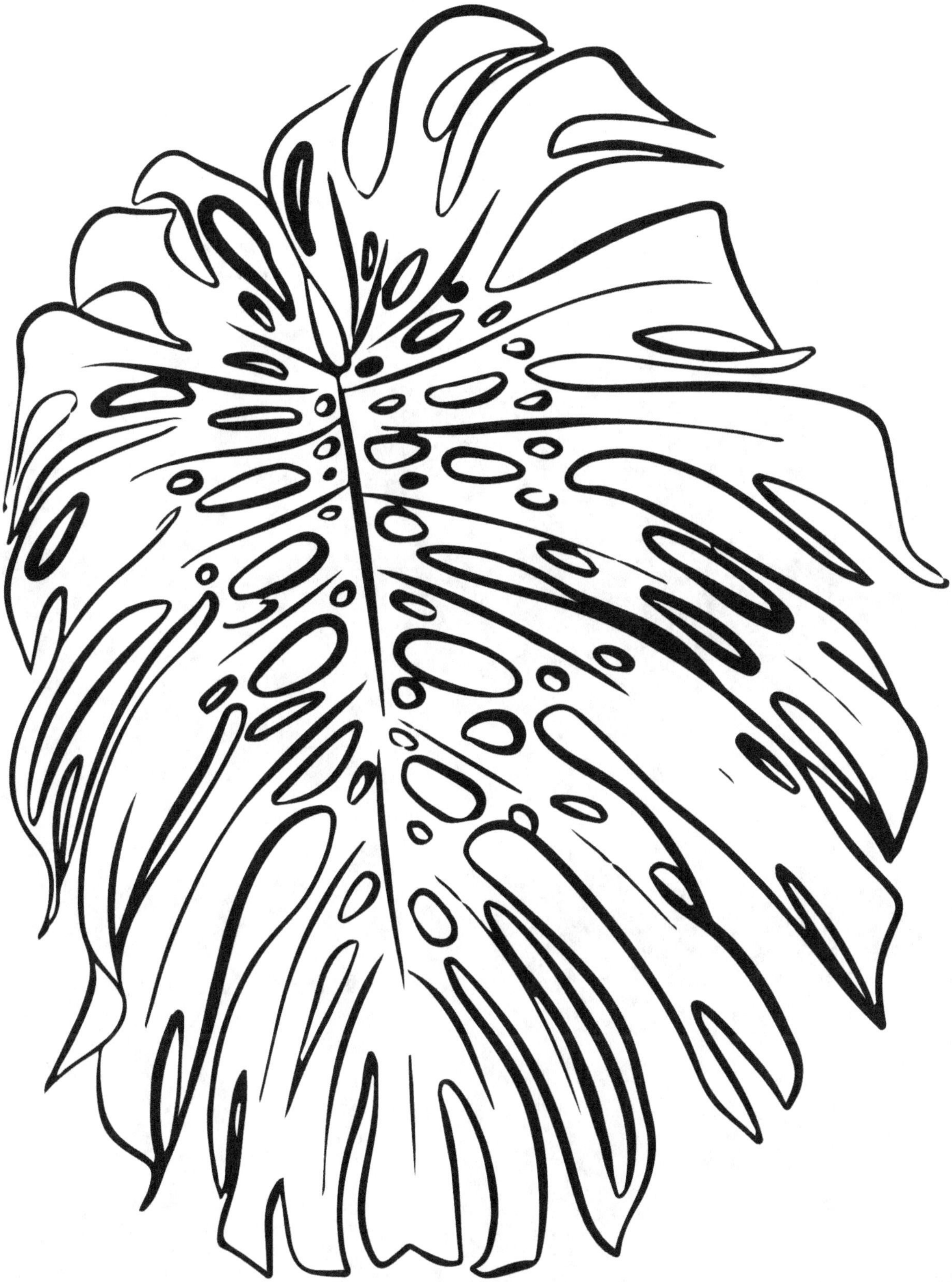

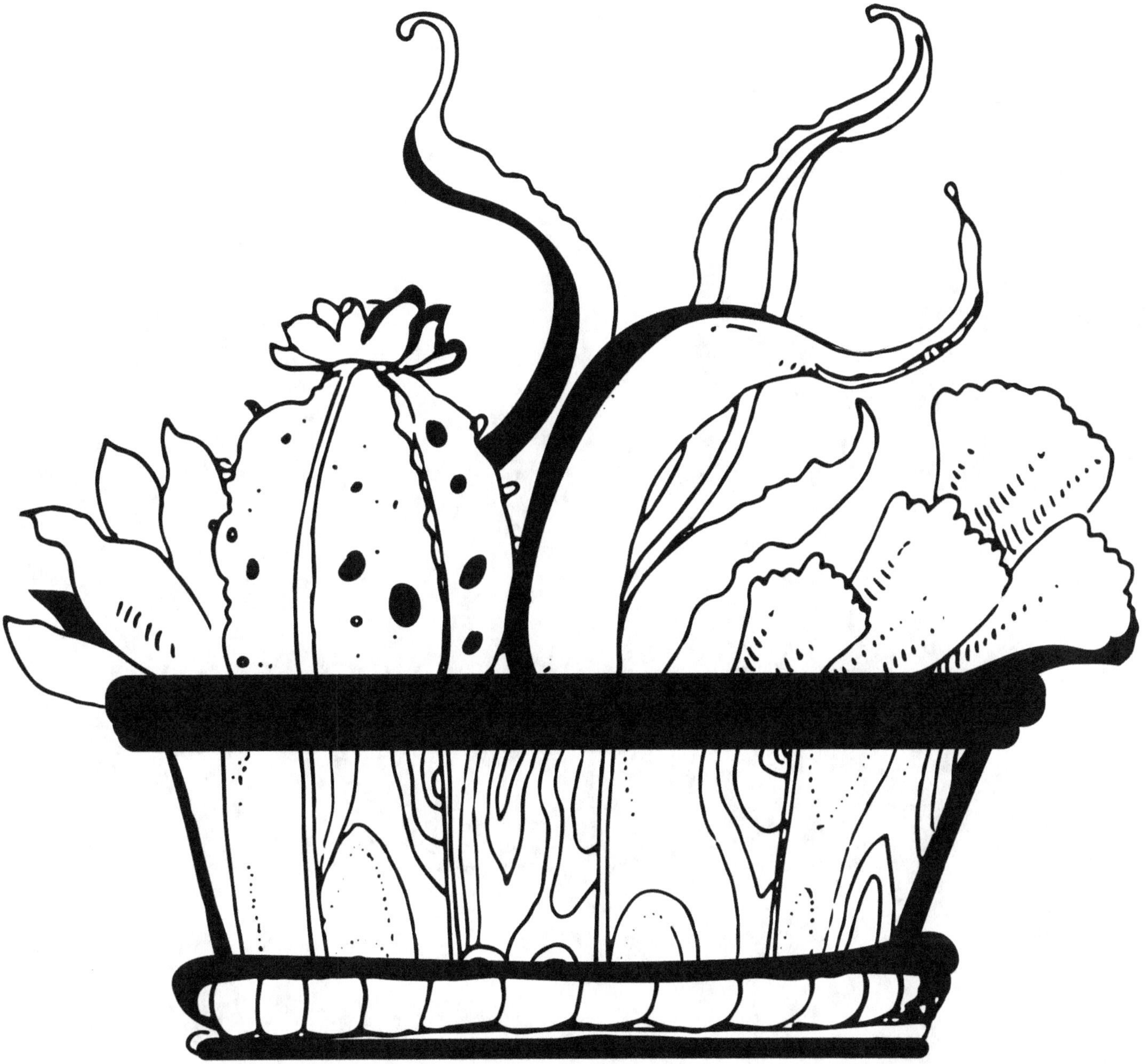

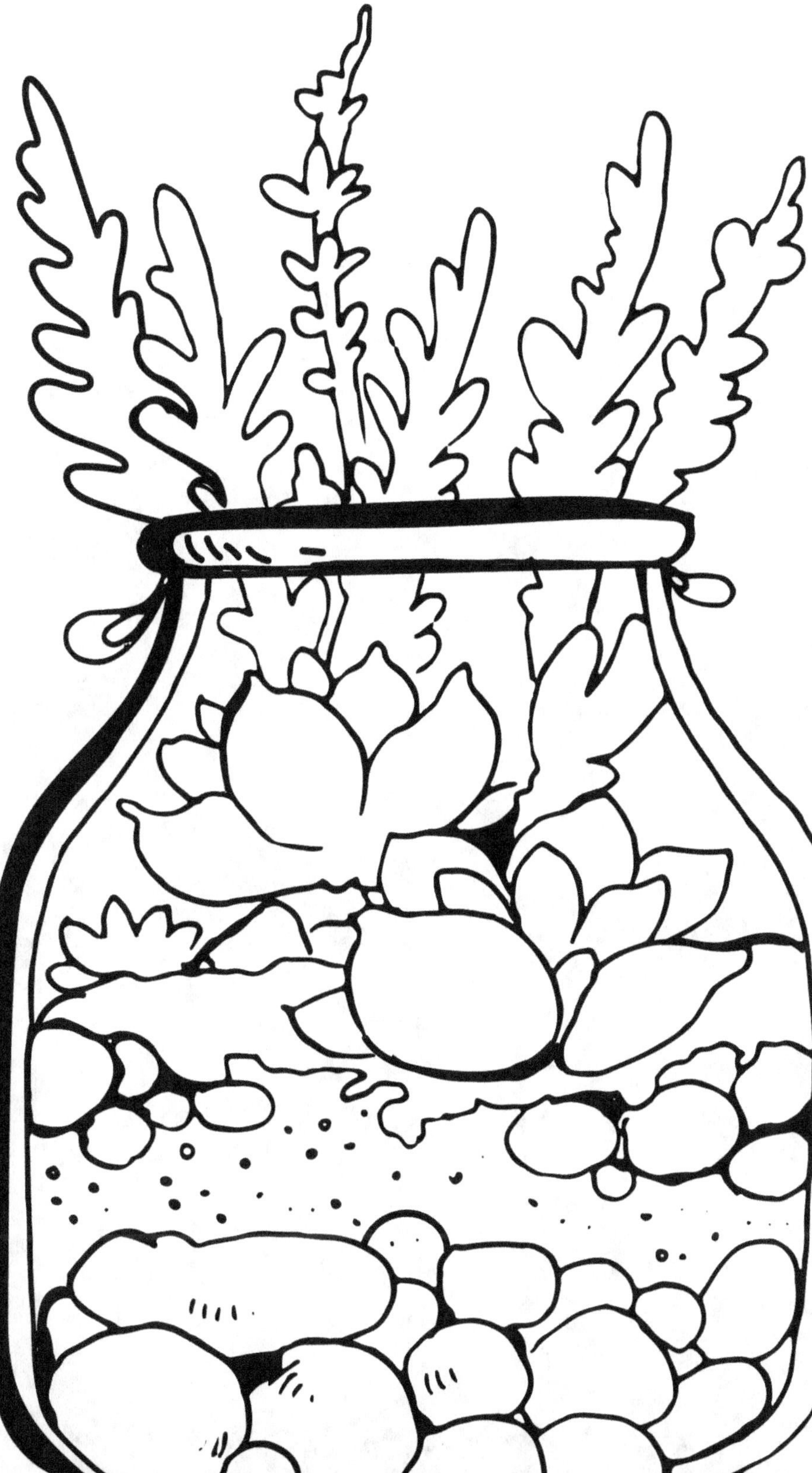

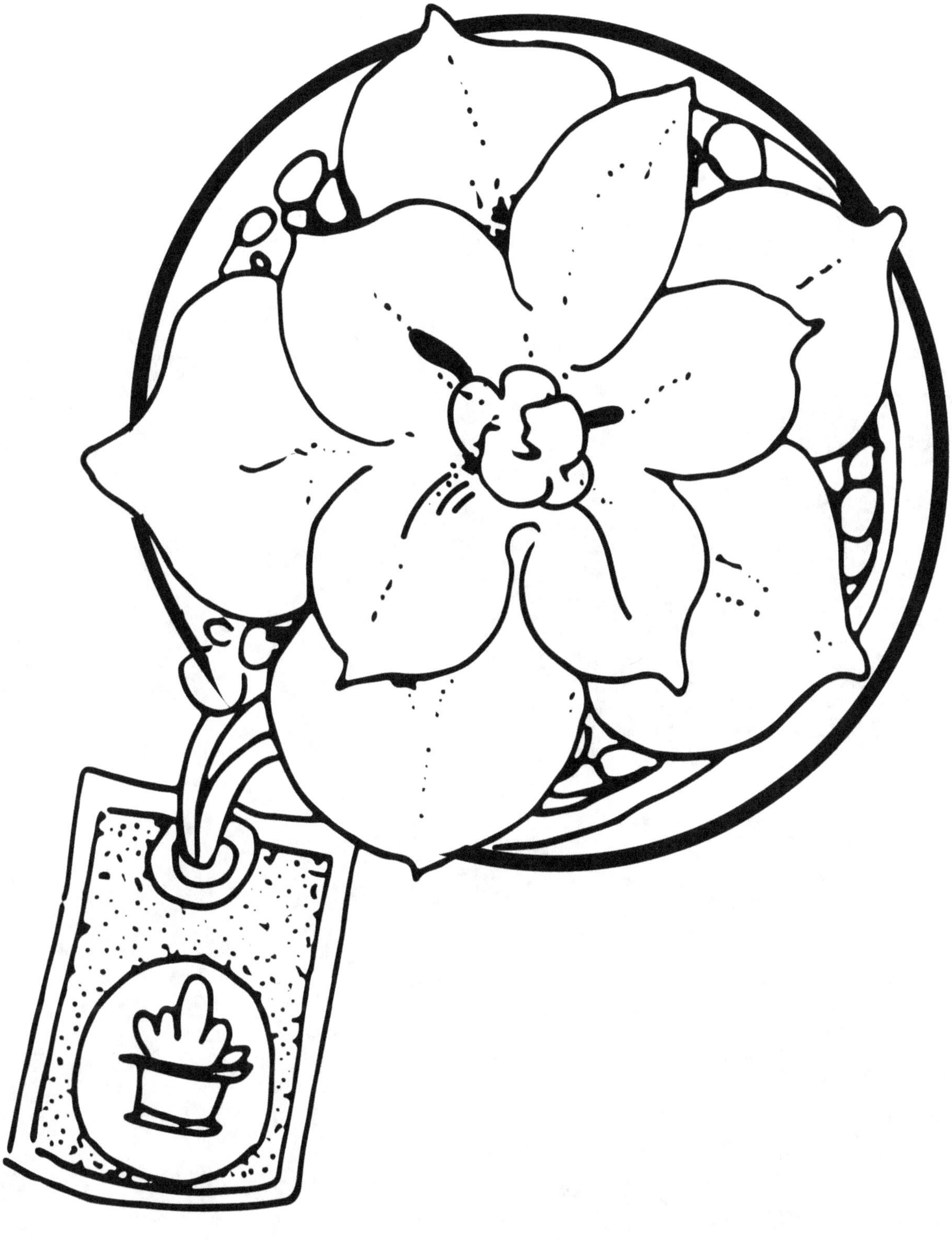

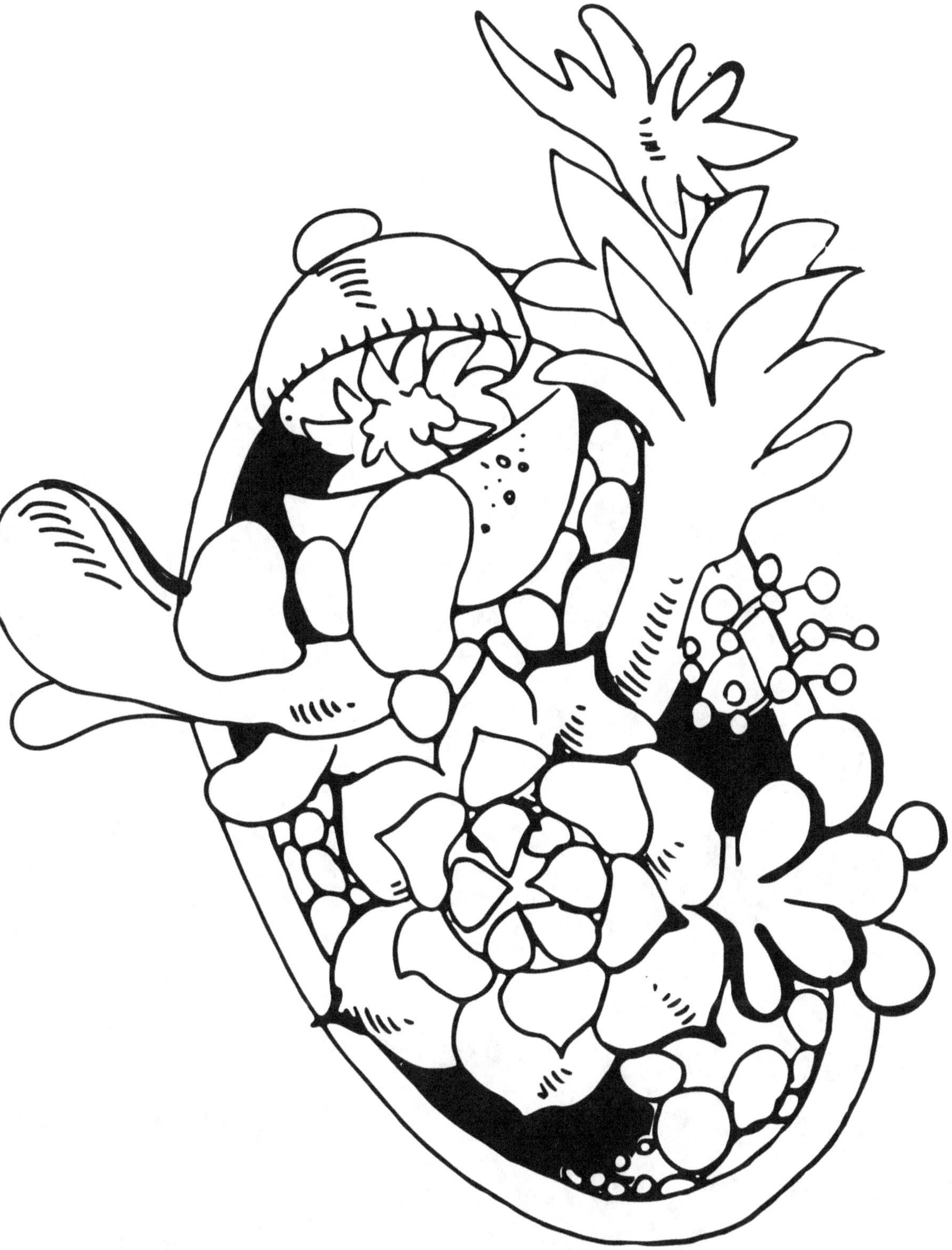

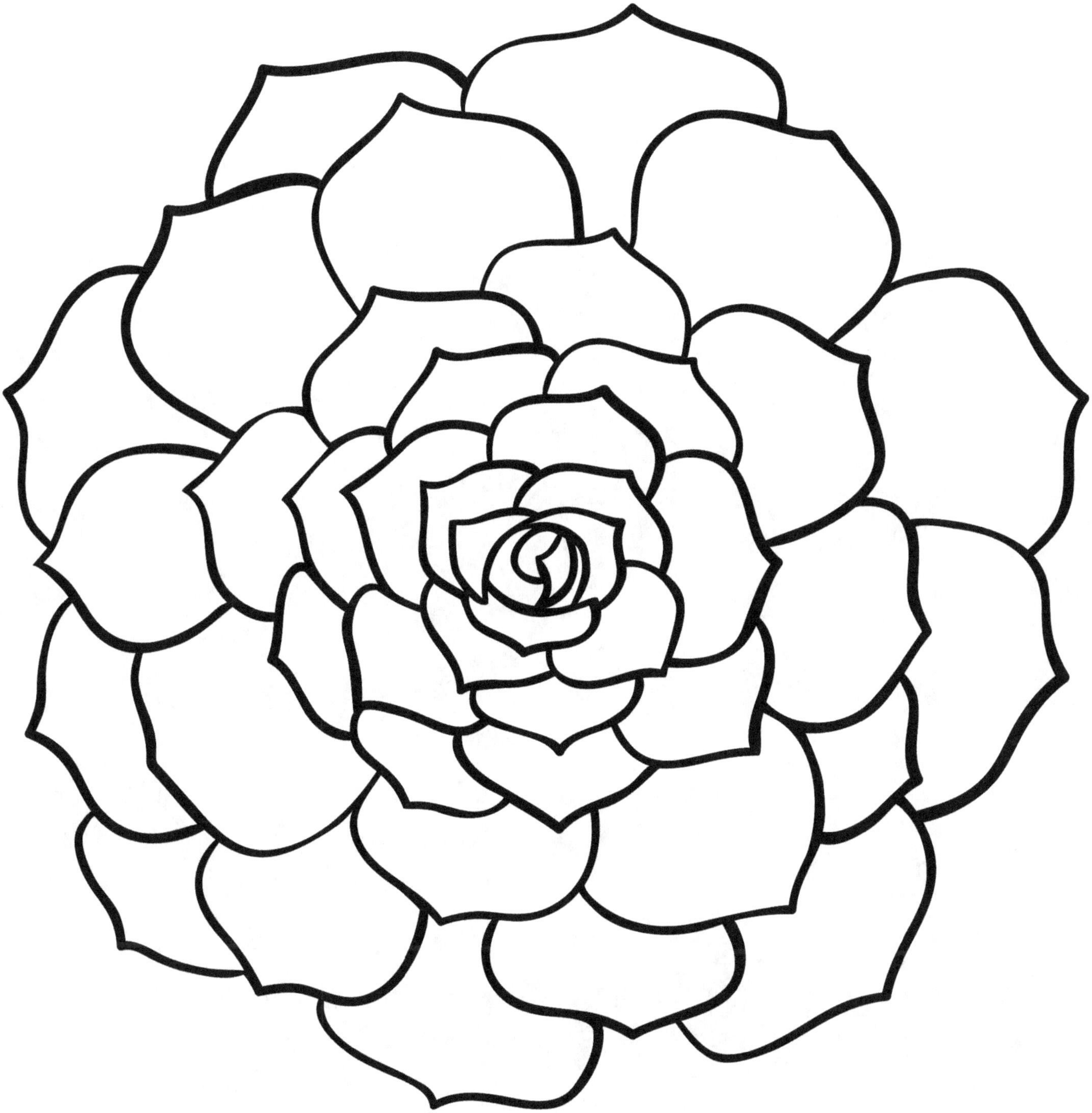

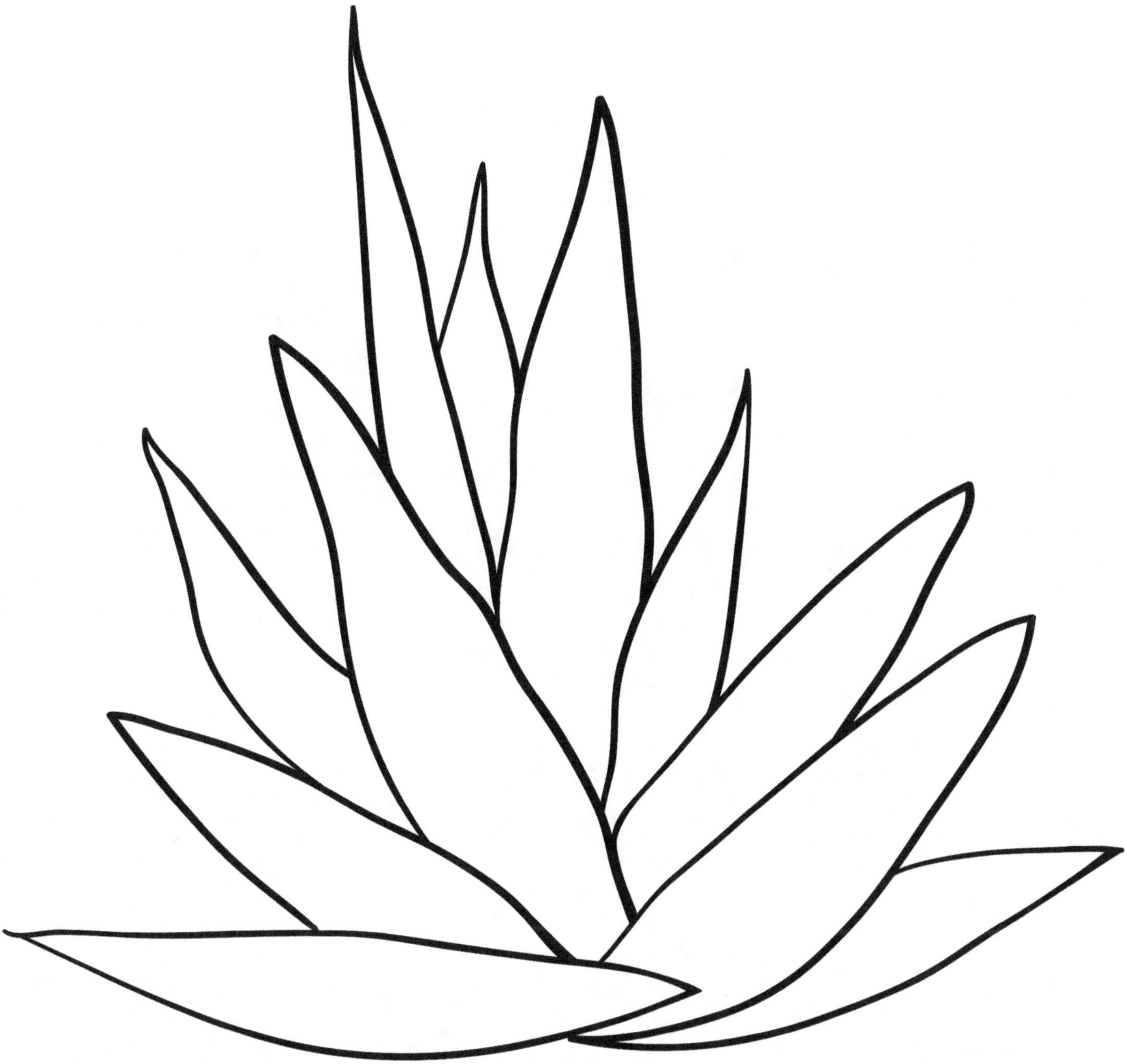

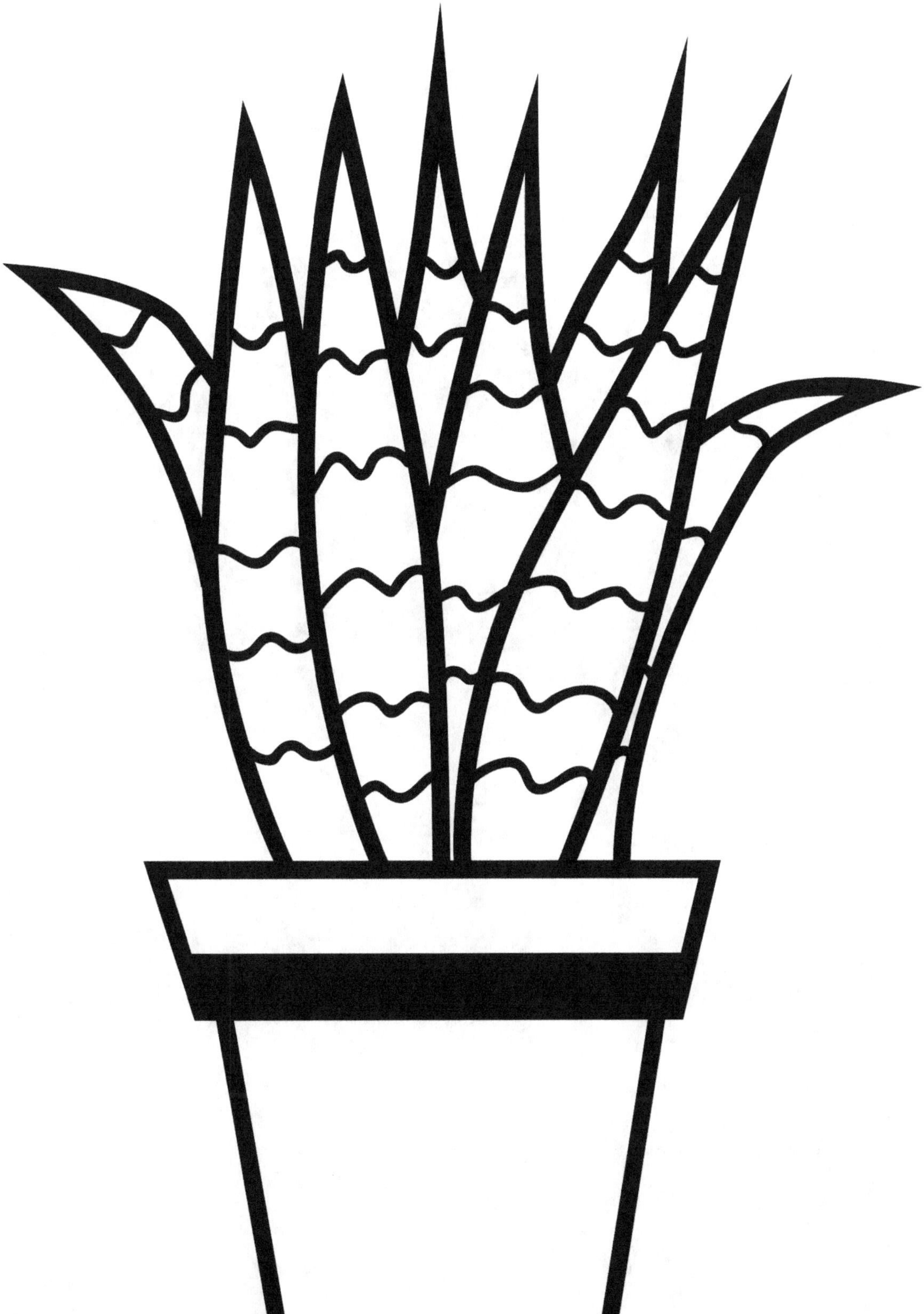

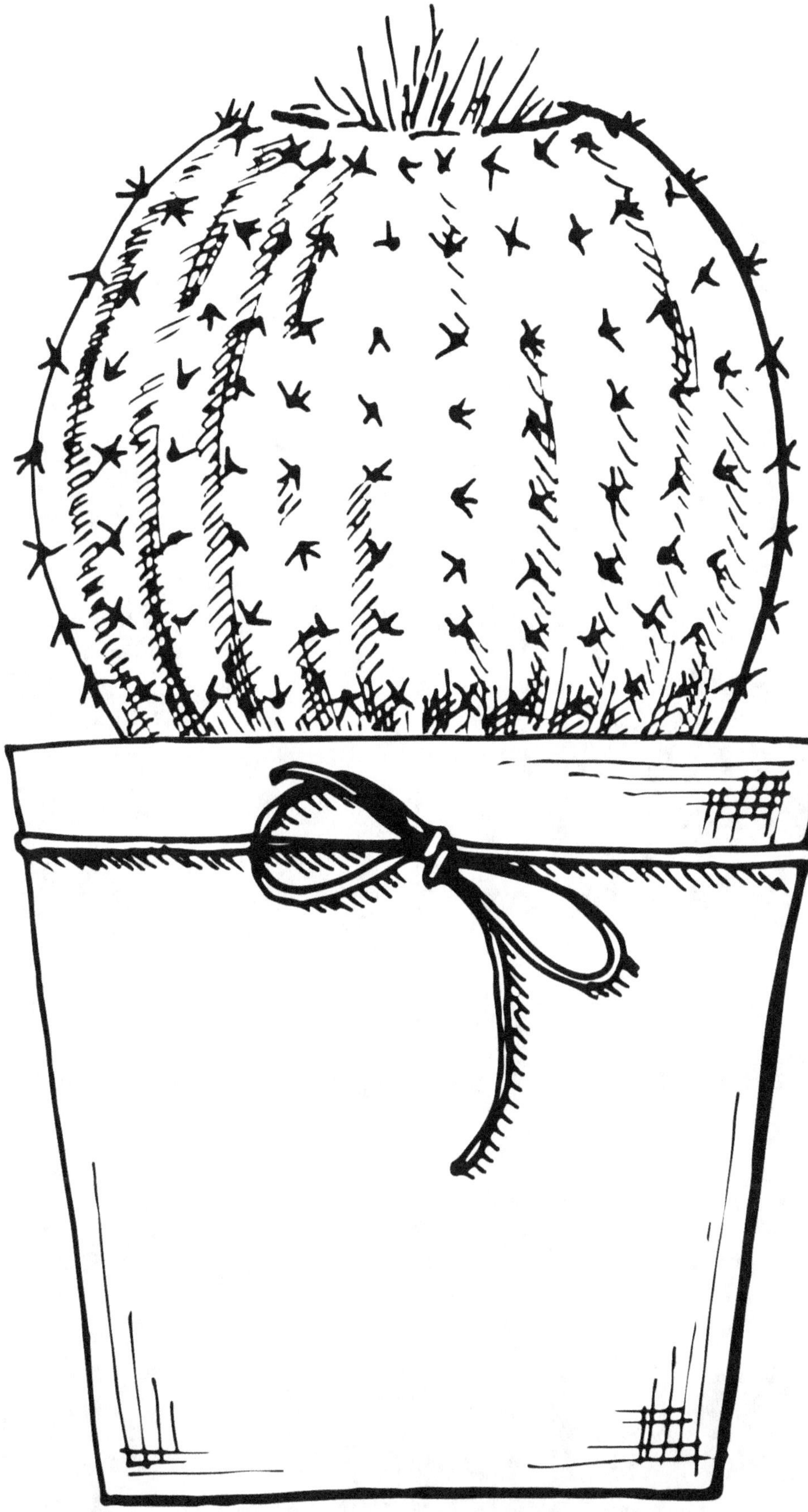

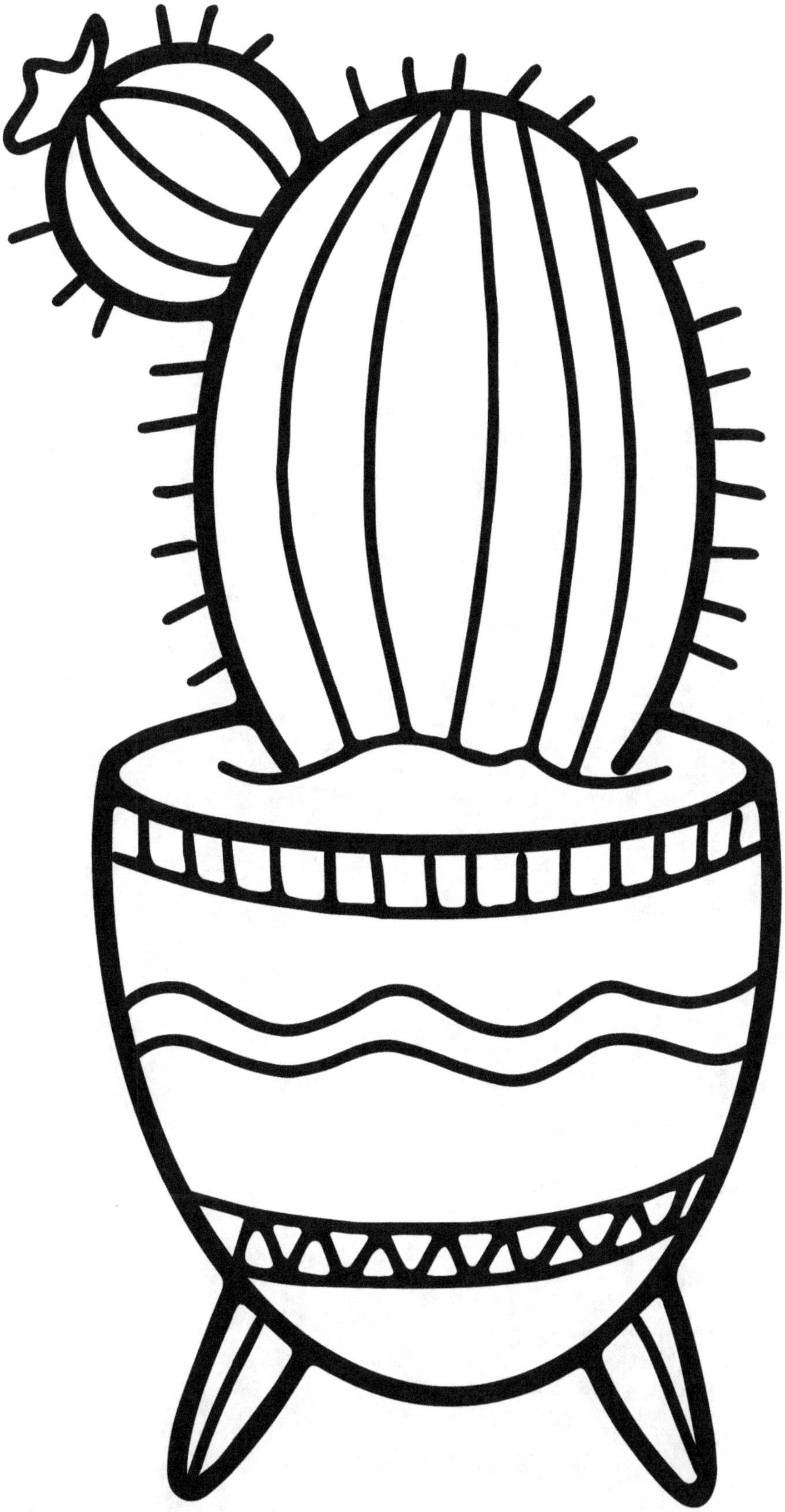

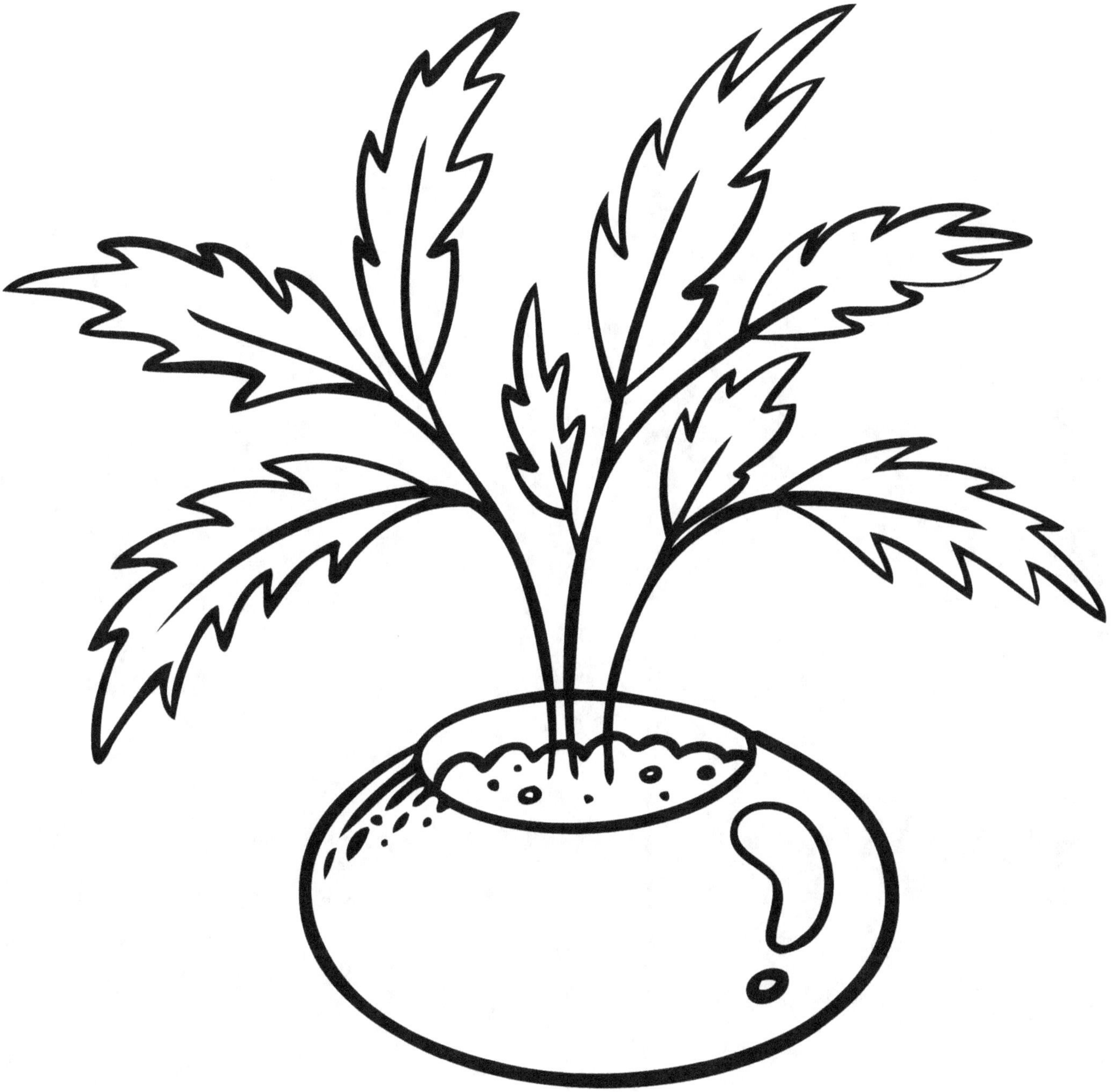

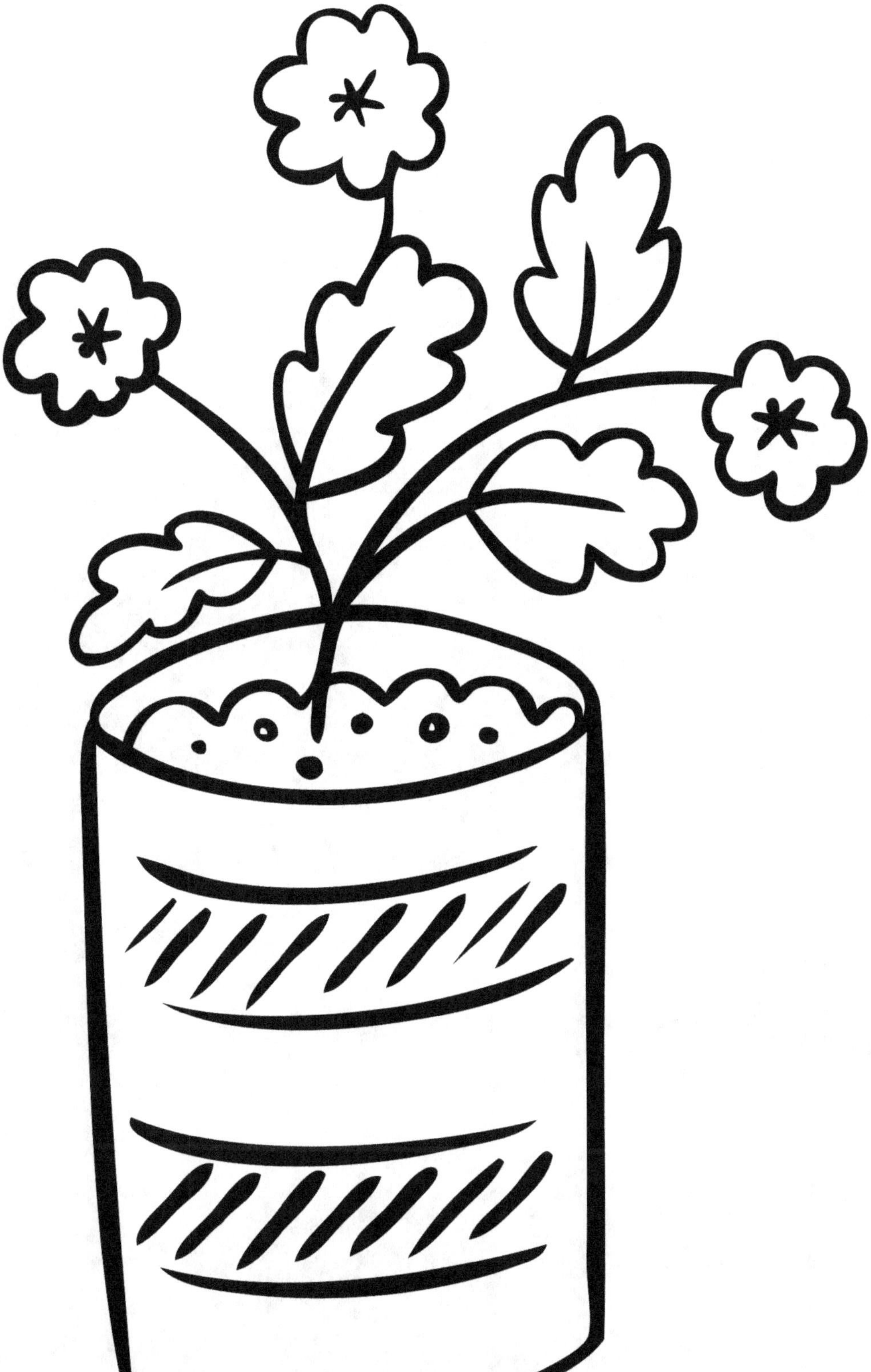

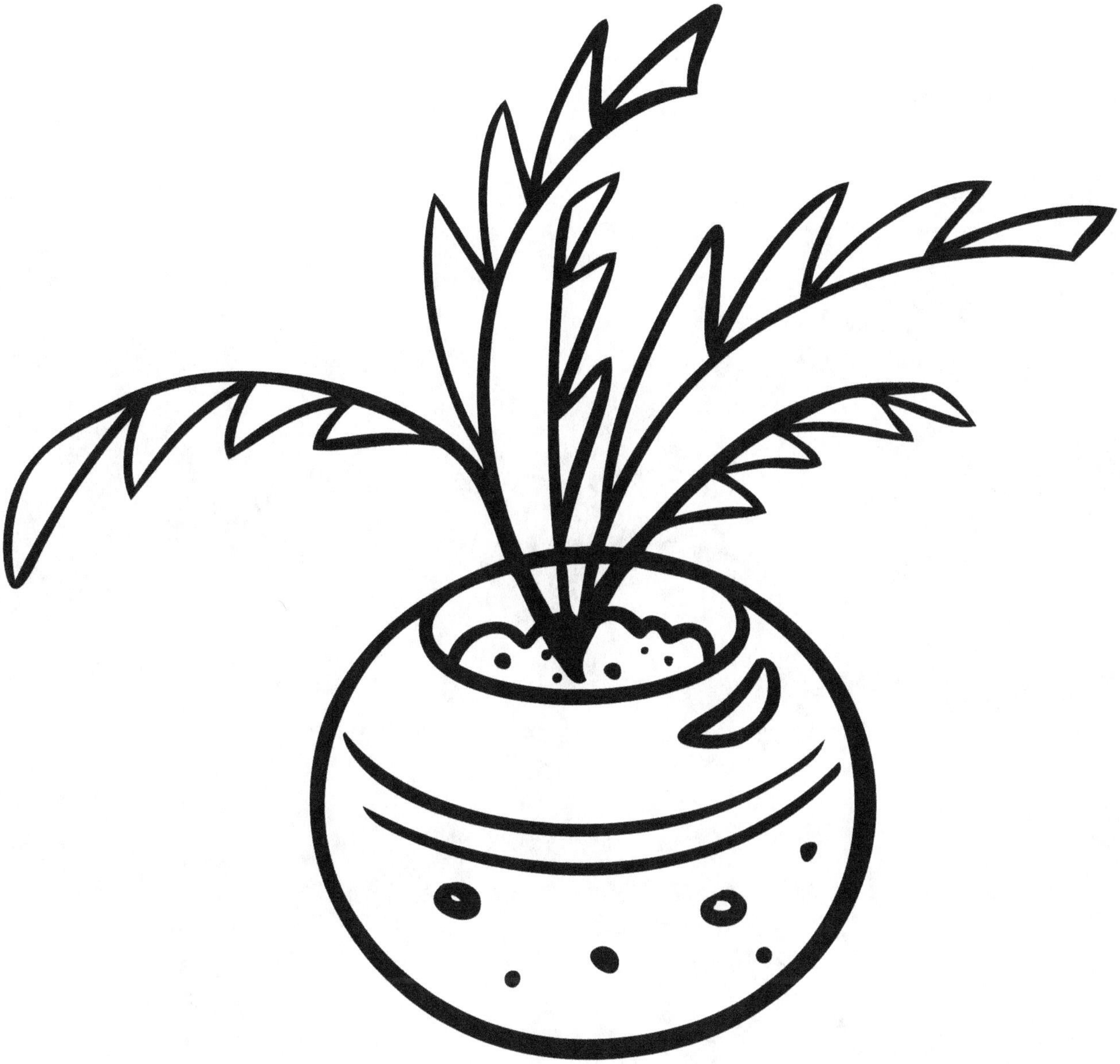

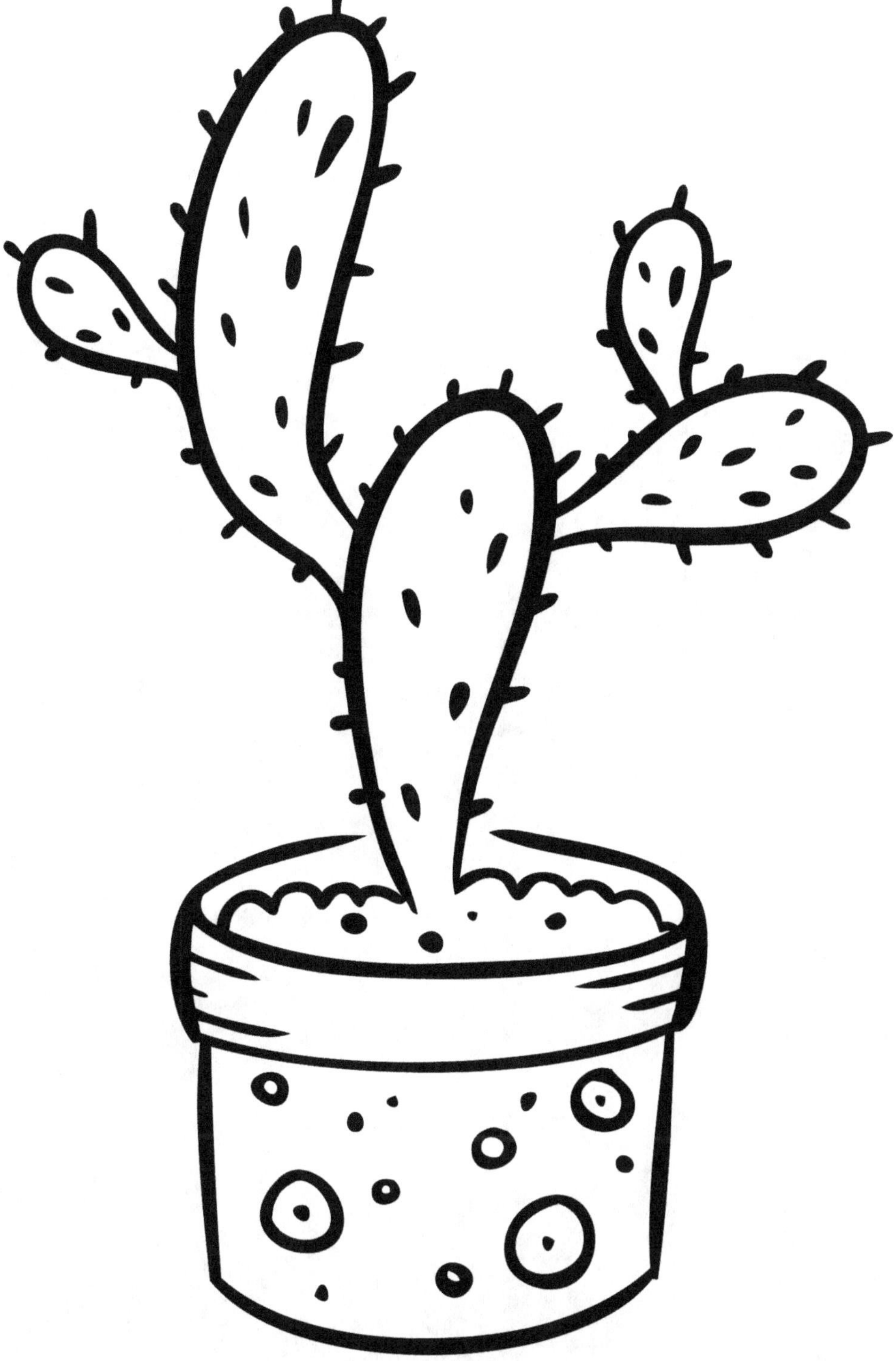

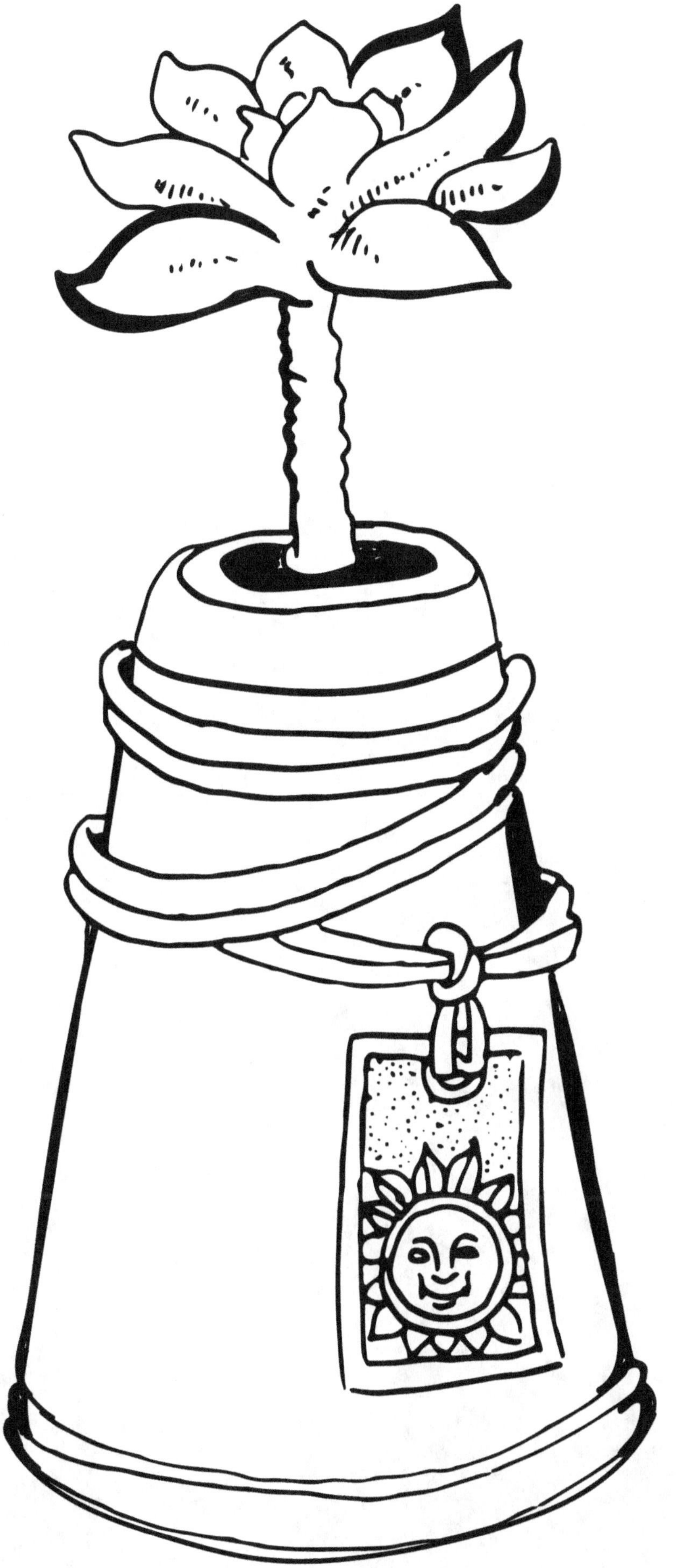

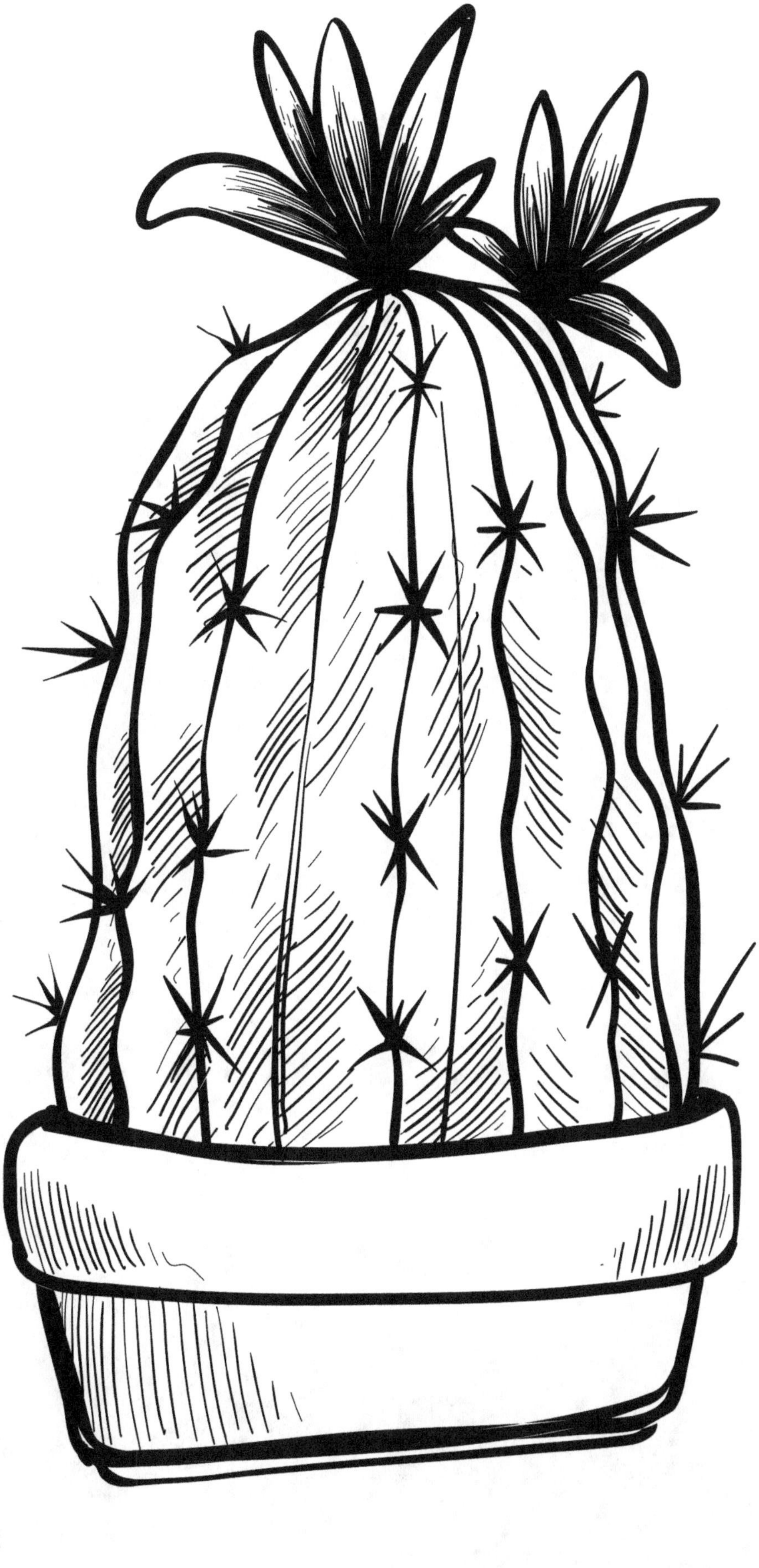

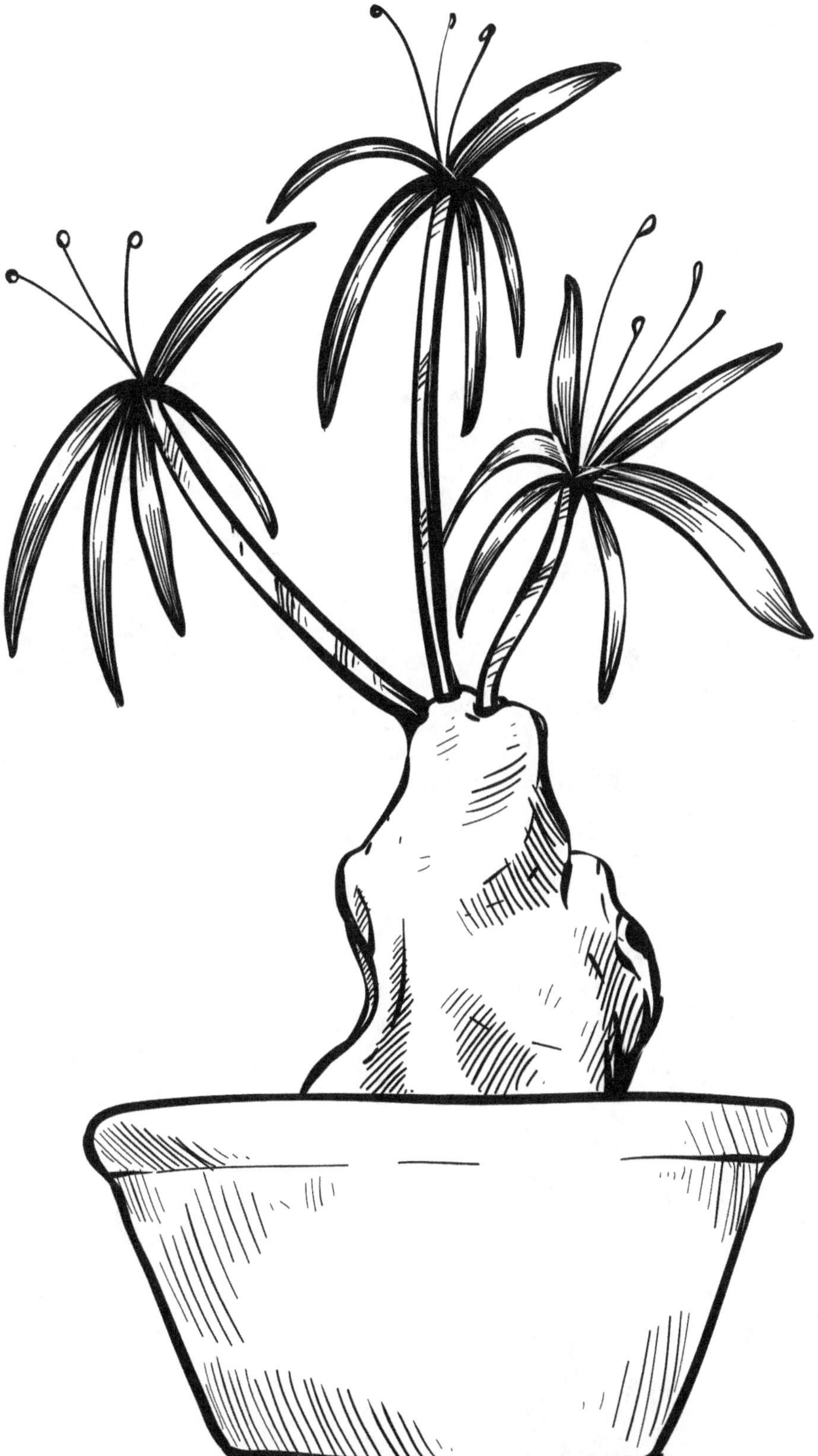

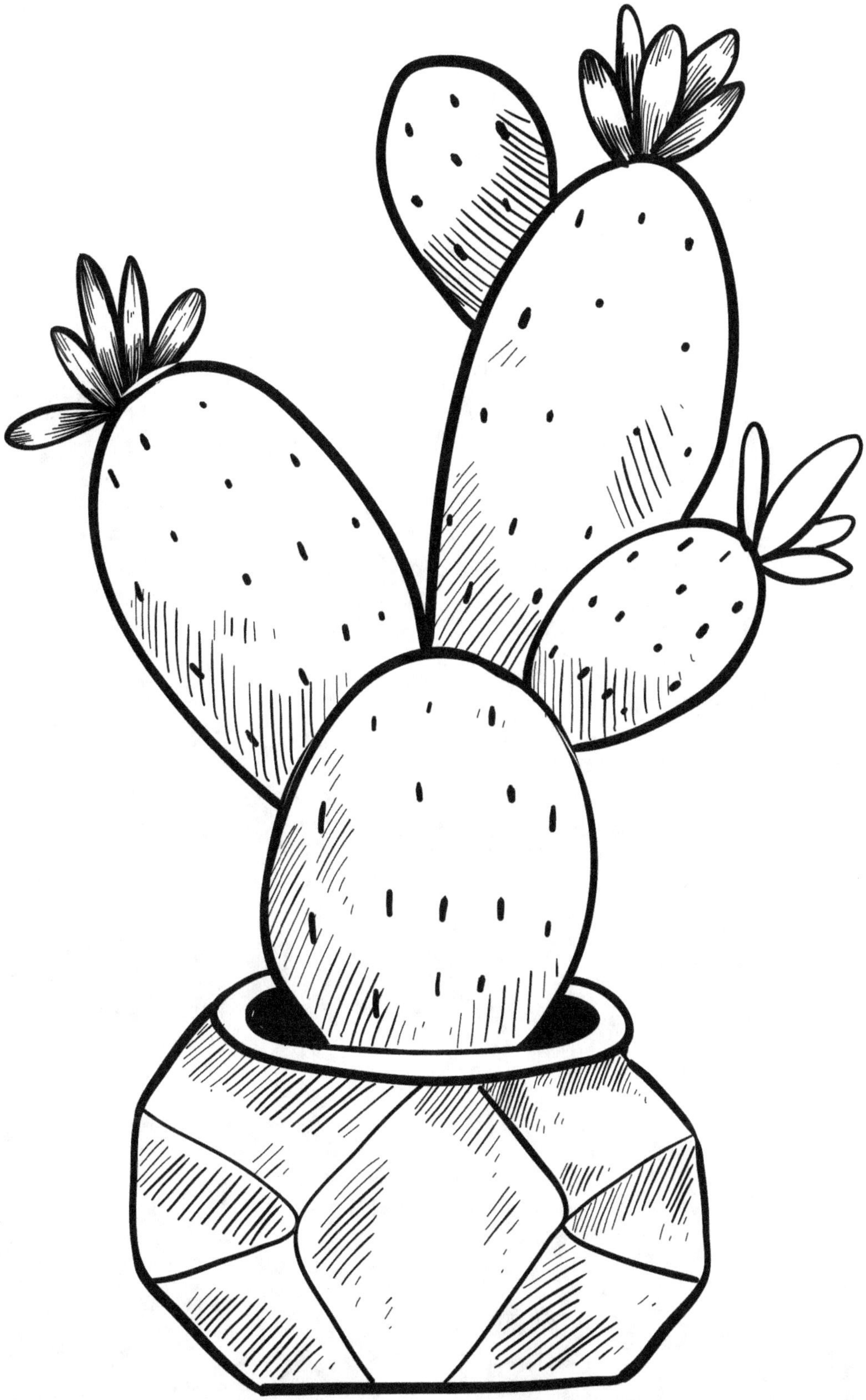

www.ingramcontent.com/pod-product-compliance
Lightning Source LLC
Chambersburg PA
CBHW080913220526
45467CB00022BA/2432
* 9 7 9 8 3 7 8 3 3 8 3 1 3 *